ANNUS HORRIBILIS

The Manure Parliament
2008 – 2009

Ann Treneman

GIBSON SQUARE

This edition published for the first time in 2009 by

Gibson Square

UK Tel: +44 (0)20 7096 1100

Fax: +44 (0)20 7993 2214

US Tel: +1 646 216 9813

Fax: +1 646 216 9488

Eire Tel: +353 (0)1 657 1057

rights@gibsonsquare.com
www.gibsonsquare.com

ISBN 978-1906142643

Printed by Clays, Bungay.

CONTENTS

Cast of Characters 4

Introduction 7
The Autumn of Discontent 17
The Winter of Much More Discontent 75
An Infernal Spring 131
The Summer of Despair 185
The Wake 241

Acknowledgements 252
Index 253

CAST OF CHARACTERS

LABOUR

Gordon Brown: Brooding, intellectual Prime Minister. Prone to car-crash politics. Said to be "psychologically flawed". Worst traits: temper (he throws phones), dithering. Nicknames: Stalin, Mr Bean, Macavity (he's not there), Great Clunking Fist.

Alistair Darling: Dull, droning Scot. A survivor who has been just about everything. Now Chancellor who has stood up to Gordon on more than one occasion. Best trait: eyebrows (birds are nesting in them). Nickname: too dull to have one.

Peter Mandelson: The man twice forced to resign under Tony Blair was reborn in autumn 2008 as Gordon Brown's confidante, becoming Baron Mandelson of Foy and Hartlepool. Wields mega-power. Thin-skinned. Best trait: fabulously silky manner. Nicknames: Prince of Darkness, Machiavelli, the Real Deputy Prime Minister.

Jacqui Smith: The first female Home Secretary (rtd). Ex-schoolteacher and former Chief Whip more famous for her expenses and her cleavage than any actual policies. Best trait: nothing comes to mind. Nickname: "Bathplug".

Harriet Harman: Dogmatic feminist elected as Labour's deputy leader. Hated by many, adored by the Volupts, an all-female group of MPs. Best trait: never briefs against others, rare in politics. Nickname: Hattie the Harpie, Harriet Harperson.

Hazel Blears: Communities Secretary (rtd): Fiery redhead who crashed in May after badly timed resignation involving a badge that said: "Rocking the boat". Best slogan: Nuts about Hazel. Nicknames: Chirpy Chirpy Cheep-Cheep, Duracell Bunny.

John McFall: Dour dry-witted Scot, head of the Treasury Select Committee, determined to make his name as the man who called the Masters of the Universe to account. It didn't quite turn out that way but he did his best.

TORIES

David Cameron: The real heir to Blair. Etonian. Keen cyclist who has recast the Tory party as the caring sharing New Conservatives. Seen as shallow, also brutal. Best trait: ability to look clean. Nicknames: Dave, Mr Sunshine, Little Lord Fauntleroy.

George Osborne. Quick-witted Shadow Chancellor with a scorpion-like streak of political malevolence. Hated by Labour and Lib-Dems alike. Wallpaper heir. Best trait: mischievous. Nickname: Boy George, Georgie Porgie.

OTHERS

Nick Clegg: Smoothie leader of the Lib-Dems. Looks too much like Dave. Good political strategist but no one remembers anything he has ever said except that he's slept with 30 women. Nickname: Clegg-Over.

Vince Cable: the only Lib-Dem who matters. The trusted voice of sanity in the credit crunch. Best trait: ability to concoct pithy phrase. Nickname: In-Vince-Able.

Michael Martin: Chippy Glaswegian Speaker (rtd). Former sheet-metal worker. Elected as Speaker for now unfathomable reasons in 2000. Nickname: Gorbals Mick.

Joanna Lumley: Beloved British actress, best known for roles in New Avengers and Absolutely Fabulous. Fierce campaigner for Gurkha rights — her father served with them — who took on the government. Best trait: sultry voice. Nickname: La Lumley.

INTRODUCTION

Why Things Could Only Get Worse

It was the fag-end of a tumultuously turbulent political year when Gordon Brown called his final press conference at Downing Street in late July, just before heading off for what is hilariously called his summer "break" but which is, of course, really just working from Scotland. At the time he was choking on the political heat and dust of Afghanistan and helicopters, the latest fiasco in a long year of political discontent. By the way, when I say long, I don't mean it (well, this IS politics). In politics, a year is just 11 months long, from September through July as August simply doesn't exist in any kind of real way.

I'm not sure what to call the events of the previous "year", for highlights will not do and "lowlights" is entirely too tame. It was a time of new nadirs, a roller-coaster that kept plunging, spirals of despair that, at times, went viral. Here, in no particular order, is an incomplete list of the year's "thrills".

The Recession. MPs expenses. Duck houses. Swine flu. Gurkhas. Fred 'the Shred' Goodwin's pension. Hazel Blears's properties. Budgetary black holes. Mandy's Royal Mail plan. Jacqui Smith's bathplug. The Speaker's resignation. Etcetera.

Given these circumstances, the question put to Gordon Brown was almost gentle. "Prime Minister," asked James Lyons, the man from the *Mirror*, "you have talked about the tough year that you've had and that the country's had with the recession, swine flu, expenses scandal and everything else. One might almost say an annus horribilis. Are you optimistic that the next 12 months ahead are going to better for you and for the country?"

As he heard the words "annus horribilis", the PM's eyes widened and his mouth formed into an instant little rosebud, an almost camp moue of surprise. As an expert on Gordon Brown facial expressions, I knew this was a genuine one. Clearly the idea that this had been his worst ever year in politics was an entirely new concept for our PM. I watched his amazement in amazement. It is bad enough to have lived through such a year — but to not know you have lived through what you have lived through shows a lack of awareness which, in itself, was another new low.

The PM now put forward an alternative view, a sort of Not The Annus Horribilis Year in Review. It had been, he allowed, a "difficult" year. "We've had to make tough decisions and we've had to make tough choices." The PM loves the word "tough". It is up there as one of his all time comfort phrases which include "this recession is global". He added: "We have taken the toughest possible decisions on banking, we have taken the toughest possible decisions on regulation, we've brought the G20 together in London so that we can deal with the economic crisis." He had also taken action on MPs expenses. “So tough decisions have been made.”

Tough. Tough. Tough. Actually I don’t think much of it was particularly tough (Fred the Shred’s pension is still safe, I believe) but, as ever with Gordo, it’s too exhausting to get bogged down in what is true and what is not. For me, it is terrifying enough to know that this is how he thinks. I get the feeling that he may say this to himself in mirror every morning. Indeed, I often imagine the PM having breakfast with Sarah (looking fragrant, as always, even as she Twitters). “Sarah, we must make tough decisions on breakfast. No more poached eggs!” Sarah, glowing, nods appreciatively (Twitter: “We’re cracking down on poached eggs at No 10! Stay tuned!”)

Back at the press conference, Gordon was still niggling away at the idea that this had been his annus horribilis. “This has not been the most difficult year for me,” he mused. “It has been a difficult year.” A difficult year? Does this mean Christmas is just a bit commercial or Moscow a trifle nippy in the winter? I tried to imagine what he could mean. I suppose he could be referring obliquely to his own personally traumatic years. Or perhaps he really believes there have been more difficult years politically. Perhaps the long years of opposition or, even, that fabled Granita pact with Tony Blair of May 1994. It all seemed quite fantastical, really, but then Gordon-land and Oz have much in common.

Gordo, warming to his theme, said: “And it is a difficult year that I think you can see that we are coming through by Building Britain’s Future, taking the decisions for the long term.” At the words “Building Britain’s Future”, I felt the desire to ring the political equivalent of NHS Direct. If our future depends on the ideas in this document, Gordo’s cobbled together “strategic plan” for saving the nation from his own rule, things are even worse than I thought. Gordo, who isn't called Stalin for nothing, was enthusiastic: "The idea that this government is not putting forward policies for the long term is completely wrong. Look at what we have done on social care, look what we have done on low-carbon technology, look at our schools White Paper, look at our action on youth employment, look at our initiative on nuclear disarmament for the rest of the world. In all these areas, we are taking action."

Social care? Low carbon technology? Surely these are words of madness. If you only skimmed them — and I don't blame you — then it bears re-skimming, if only to marvel at the scale of denial. It makes you realise that things are, actually, worse than you thought. Indeed, if it wasn't all so real, it would be hilarious. This is denial that is almost up there with Saddam's media illusionist, Comical Ali who, while standing on a hotel roof, declared, as Iraqi troops fled for cover behind him: "Baghdad is safe. Don't believe those liars."

So Britain is safe. We are Building Britain's Future. Later in the press conference (if you don't think a year is a long time in politics, just try living through one press conference), for no apparent reason, he returned to his alternative view of the year. Here is Gordo, unplugged: "I was asked was it the toughest year I've faced, I don't think so. I've faced tougher years, but equally, at the same time, have we made the right decisions? Have we made decisions based on our belief about what is right for the country?" He stopped for a nano-second before concluding that, actually, yes, he HAD made the right decisions. "If you look back on all the things that we've done: we've made decisions on nuclear; we've made decisions on planning; we've made decisions on climate change; we've made decisions on expanding the education leaving age to 18;

we've made decisions to change the nature of regulation for the banks; we've made decisions to rescue the banks by recapitalising them, not simply by providing liquidity; we've made decisions at the G20 to go for growth in the world economy; and we've made decisions in the last few weeks in Building Britain's Future to take seriously the new industries and the new skills that we need."

As he spoke, the economy was in deep trouble, Afghanistan in flames, unemployment rising, politicians close to meltdown but, hey ho!, details, details. And yet STILL he would not stop, continuing at length about his wonderful agenda. OK. I hear your pain and I'm going to stop quoting Gordo now but there is method in my madness. For I do this to illustrate how the PM had made his annus horribilis much more horribilis than it needed to be because of his political personality. By that I mean his endless self-justification, his lists, his false comparisons, his dogmatism, his almost visceral need to be right at all times. Indeed, I'm surprised, he didn't announce that, actually, 2009 hadn't been nearly as bad as 1349 (The Black Death), 1536 (Henry VIII at his worst) and 1812 (when the PM was murdered). Nor has it helped that he is pitted against Tory leader David Cameron, who may seem as shallow as a puddle but, especially when it came to MPs' expenses, proved to be strategically brilliant if brutal.

Looking back, the most remarkable thing about politics in 2009 is how it kept getting worse. In September 2008, Alistair Darling was treated like a pariah by Downing Street when he dared to suggest that this could be the worst recession in 60 years. It wasn't long before that was seen as rose-tinted optimism. By February, Schools Secretary Ed Balls, Gordon's mini-me, was saying the recession was the worst for "probably more than 100 years". Other things that kept hitting new extremes included the national debt, Labour's popularity, the May election results (the worst ever for Labour). And I haven't even got to MPs expenses with their moats and mortgages.

It's strange because I had remembered the whole year as being ghastly for the PM. But then I started to sift through my sketches from last September for this book. It was interesting how when put together these daily snapshots — which are often written in a tearing hurry and published the next day in *The Times* — provide a picture which is much more than the sum of its parts. The thing you get in sketches that you don't get anywhere else is the detail. So think of this book as a funny peculiar kind of historical collage. For it was only after all the sketches of key events were chosen, edited and topped with mini-introductions, that I began to see the true (pear) shape of the year.

Actually, Gordon had a pretty good autumn. OK, so for the world, it was an economic disaster but Labour's poll ratings did rise, as recorded by Populus, to within four points of the Tories in early December. It was like a reverse halo effect: the disastrous global economy made Gordo look good. I mean that figuratively for, of course, he looked terrible, which was part of his appeal at the time. Dave seemed, if possible, even shallower. The Lib-Dems ... well, who cares, really, except for Vince Cable who, at times, seemed the only one making sense in a caddywampus world.

But the Autumn of Discontent led to a winter of even deeper discontent and a spring and summer of total meltdown. The events just kept coming. It felt like we were all trying to find the bottom of one of those bottomless lakes: just when you thought it couldn't get any worse, it did and then, the next day, it got worse again. The stories were incredible. From a sketch-writing point of view, I wasn't sure that anyone could improve on the Home Secretary, Jacqui Smith, with her claim for her 88p bathplug and £10 porn films for her husband. But then there was the moat and the duck houses and Little Hazie Blears and her various homes and, well, the madness just went on

The strangest moment? It had to be in April with Gordon Brown gurning and swaying on YouTube as he explained his latest wizard wheeze to pay MPs extra for coming to work. He looked quite close to bonkers. Or there was the day that the Absolutely Fabulous actress Joanna Lumley appeared to be running the country. Still, to cheer us up, there was the fabulous apparition that is Baron Mandelson of Foy and Hartlepool. Who would have dreamt, at the beginning of the year, that Peter M could be so reinvented. Or Alan Sugar! Some insist that day that Sirallun joined the team (giving birth to a million "You're hired!" headlines) was the true new nadir.

It is easy to see this year as an entry in a freak show which, like a Diane Arbus photograph, endlessly fascinates even as it repels. But what matters, in politics, is not so much what happens but how leaders react. For a time, the recession worked for Gordon but, as things worsened in the country and as various details, like Sir Fred's obscenely generous pension arrangements became public, the boasting from Number 10 began to grate. Looking back, and especially reading the detailed quotes from these sketches, you can see how Gordon sowed the seeds of his own destruction. And how, in the depths of winter, David Cameron began to turn it round, heating up the debate on debt, nationalisation, honesty and leadership. He used Gordon's words against him and, like errant landmines, they began to explode. It truly takes some kind of reverse political genius to lay a field of landmines for yourself, as our PM did.

Then there was the eX-factor. The issue of MPs' expenses had been bubbling away like one of those stinking sulphurous mud pools for years but, after the Commons lost a High Court battle to disclose the expenses, it was finally coming to a head. Various stories emerged in the spring and in early May the *Daily Telegraph* began what would be a month of revelations. What did Gordon do? Not much really. As the nation fumed, Gordo dithered. But David Cameron launched himself at the issue like an Exocet missile, forcing his front benchers to pay money back. He himself paid back the £680 he'd claimed to trim his wisteria, grovelling all the way. He talked tough and, crucially, acted tough. Shallow Dave had, it seemed, hidden depths.

Truth be told, Gordo, obsessed with the global economy, probably saw all of this as a bit of a parochial sideshow. He misjudged this and much else including Gurkhas, 42-days detention, Afghanistan, the Royal Mail and later, during the summer break, the explosive issue of Libya. Then, as the new political year dawned, he stepped on another of his own landmines, his endless insistence earlier in the year that the choice for voters would be "Labour investments versus Tory cuts". But even now, with the footprints still fresh in the fabled sands of time, it can be seen how Gordon could have turned it round: less hubris, more honesty, an apology or two, less time in the bunker, much much less dithering, more eX-factor action, more openness and a few laughs too. But, of course, he didn't turn it round. Dave did.

So pay no attention to Gordon Brown and his protestations that, actually, 2009 wasn't really so bad. Read these sketches and remember, remember, it WAS that bad. Indeed, worse. There is no denying it. For the lesson of 2008-2009 is that just when you think that things can't get any worse, they do. Labour once sang that things can only get better. Actually, we now know the truth: this was the year when things could only get worse — and they did. Politics really will never be the same again.

Ann Treneman
London
28 September 2009

THE AUTUMN OF DISCONTENT

The political year dawned with Gordon Brown on the rocks after a fractious summer of criticism from rebellious MPs. Any talk of a coup collapsed, though, as the full horror of the economic crisis became apparent (Lehman Brothers would fall on 15 September). Gordon galloped to the rescue and, for a few fleeting weeks, he did, actually, seem to be saving the world. Peter Mandelson, now wearing ermine, couldn't keep the smile off his face. But it couldn't last…

3 September
A teeny tiny relaunch

Gordon Brown returned to Downing Street with his premiership in the doldrums and the latest Populus poll showing Labour 16 points behind the Tories. His Chancellor was in the doghouse over his candid remarks on the recession. In the circumstances, there was only one thing to do — relaunch!

The Great Gordo Relaunch had been heavily hyped and though I wasn't expecting fireworks (this was a relaunch, not a miracle), I was certainly expecting something. But, as the day unfolded, it became clear that the relaunch, like Hurricane Gustav, was going to have to be reclassified. By afternoon, it had almost disappeared completely, not so much a relaunch as a de-launch.

The actual day's events were a closely guarded secret as I discovered when I rang No 10 at 8.30 am. "Where's the relaunch?" I asked. Silence. A voice said there would be a statement from Hazel Blears's department. And? "The Prime Minister will be visiting a first time buyer's flat." Great! Can I come? "No. It's a small flat."

Yes, it was (for I had a spy there), but that was entirely fitting for, as we now know, it was an even smaller relaunch. Indeed it was so tiny that I wouldn't be surprised to find out that it had been organised by elves.

It all began with a "ping!" at 9.30 am when an absurdly brief Treasury e-mail arrived announcing the stamp duty holiday. It consisted of 73 words. This may be the shortest Treasury announcement ever. Where was the Chancellor? Had Gordo imprisoned him for saying the unsayable (i.e. the recession is going to be the worst in 60 years)? Perhaps Mr Darling has been handcuffed and was having to type with a pencil clamped between his teeth or, more likely, his eyebrows: certainly that would explain the brevity.

The Treasury would only say that Alistair Darling was in his office and had no plans to leave it. How ominous was that? Later he appeared on TV (hands not visible), words coming out of his mouth that he clearly did not want to say. As I type there are fears that the Chancellor remains under office arrest.

The TV image swung from Darling in a tiny corner of his office to Gordo in a tiny flat. The Prime Minister, dressed for a funeral in a dark suit, was opening and closing his mouth like a fish (no "live" words allowed at a Gordo de-launch). He was mouthing at a tousled-haired man, presumably the flat-owner, who looked thoroughly alarmed. The head of Hazel Blears (itself a terrifying object) kept popping in and out of shot.

How very modern to relaunch in a Ikea flat-pack kitchen without sound after imprisoning your Chancellor. My spy tells me that Mr Tousled had only a half hour's notice that the PM was joining him for a bowl of cereal (until then, he'd thought it was his MP). The poor guy had just moved in and hadn't even unpacked. The visit lasted all of 15 minutes, just long enough for Gordon to say some real words ("live!") on camera in front of the man's kitchen cabinets. This was Gordon as Everyman.

Outside, plucky little Hazel rabbited away as the rain bucketed down. Can it get any worse? Expect another relaunch any day now.

10 September

Darling impersonates a dead phone

The TUC conference marks the official start of the political year: this year it was the Chancellor's turn to appear before the brothers and sisters who were not amused.

Alistair Darling has always been dull. Indeed, I had not thought it possible for him to get duller. I was wrong, for Mr Darling came before us at the TUC in Brighton as the Human Drone. His mouth moved and the words coming out of it were English but, taken together, they meant nothing. Instead, they merged into one long tone, not unlike the sound of a telephone when it goes dead.

It was quite a feat and, if he loses his job as Chancellor, he may want to become a fairground attraction. The noise (it was hardly a speech) went on for 30 minutes. The comrades of the TUC, who had spent the day calling for the renationalisation of everything in Britain that isn't nailed down, treated him with politeness bordering on contempt. They sat, sullen, resentful, eyes down. As Mr Darling reached the "climax" of his speech a man on stage opened his mouth in the biggest yawn I have seen outside a zoo.

I would give you highlights but there weren't any. He did not say one thing that everybody doesn't know already. Times are tough. The credit crunch is nothing to do with this Government. "Times are tough," he said. "Together we will get through it."

Will we? I wasn't even sure I was going to get through the next half hour, much less the recession. Over the summer, Mr Darling gave an interview in front of a peaty fire in his Hebridean croft in which he seemed in danger of coming across as a rather candid human being. Clearly that phase is over. There was no trace of warmth or humour yesterday, nor any feeling that we were being told the truth about the economy. One lit match had more heat than his entire performance.

Everything about him was damped down, subdued. Even his eyebrows, which normally can be depended on to provide some light entertainment, had been tranquillised. It's amazing how he can say the words "I have said I am listening" in exactly the same way as he would say "I have said I am listening to the weather forecast" Reassuring? I don't think so.

The question-and-answer session provided the only passion of the entire non event. The comrades hissed and jeered when he said private sector pay had gone up more than in the public sector. They mocked him over his lack of energy windfall tax. Mr Darling, in his only moment of emotion, doggedly defended his policy of loft lagging. "It's easy to knock it but actually it can cut people's fuel bills," he insisted.

The applause from the Brothers Grim was parsimonious. Now I know what the sound of one and a half hands clapping sounds like. Mr Darling had been greeted by six seconds, max, of light finger tapping. During the speech there was no applause at all, which must be some kind of first. It ended with another six seconds of finger-tapping. Indeed, the only really heartfelt applause was when A. Darling, Human Drone, left the stage.

12 September

The future's bright, the future's lagging

Downing Street would prefer, if possible, for the Prime Minister never to appear in public live in front of journalists. But, since nothing else had worked so far ...

To Downing Street, then, for Gordon Brown autumn relaunch number three. Or is it four? It's hard to keep track. When the going gets tough, the tough get relaunching. Until yesterday Gordon Brown had been doing it exclusively for the TV cameras. Now he came before us in the flesh and, well, I can tell you that there is a lot less flesh now.

The PM looks as if he has lost about a stone, and it shows in his face in particular. The cheeks look almost gaunt. The jaw, always thrusting, now juts. The neck has gone a bit wattle-y, and his Minotaur head seems even larger because his shoulders are not quite as broad. He needs a new suit. Perhaps he is waiting to see if, deprived of his daily Pilates forced upon him by his wife over the summer, the weight will go back on. For the PM, the credit crunch could be the credit munch.

This was the energy relaunch. It took place in a room with 16 light bulbs, all blazing. I guess it is hard to economise when you've got chandeliers. So how many politicians does it take to change a light-bulb policy? Answer: three. There was Gordo (well, 90 per cent of him), John "Mad Eyes" Hutton and Hilary "Harry Potter" Benn. As a trio, they looked quite alarming.

Gordon's lectern bore the motto "save energy, save energy". And, also, of course, save capital letters. This is very much a lower-case relaunch. Gordon has been thinking all summer about how to counter the vertiginous rise in our utility bills. He feels our pain (he told us yet again) and now he has the answer.

We can lower our own bills. Yes, it's so simple! The PM has discovered that Britain is lagging behind on loft lagging. So Gordo has fixed it so the poor will get free loft lagging and the rest of us will get a discount. Isn't it great to be able to lower our own bills by spending more money? I can only imagine what is coming next: perhaps a national drive to get us all to buy draught excluders shaped like sausage dogs.

Gordon's other big relaunch idea is direct debits. He wants to "actively promote" the use of direct debits. It was all about lasting change. "Our objective is nothing less than a sea-change in energy efficiency and consumption." As he said this, I noticed the empty room behind him was also fully lit.

I don't know if it's the effect of all those Pilates classes or what (drugs?) but the PM was very calm and collected. He remains completely convinced of his own superior decision making. "I made the right decision last autumn," he announced about his decision not to call an election.

Oh, and he was right on the economy, nuclear power, planning reform, climate change and so on. But, he was asked, do you ever have a dark night of the soul and think, "Actually, I'm the problem"?

This brought muted giggles from the hacks and one of Gordo's terrifyingly white smiles (I actually saw a lightbulb glinting off one of his front teeth).

"Go around the world!" he cried. "Talk to any president in any country and talk about how government is having to deal with what is a completely unique situation. Our job is to take people through this!"

When it was over, Gordon strode out of the room. He didn't, however, turn out the lights.

16 September
In-Vince-ible Vince

Lehman Brothers was crashing and burning as the Lib-Dems met for their conference in Bournemouth. This only allowed Vince to shine even more.

Vince Cable — rock star! Well, the closest the Lib Dems will ever get to one. Honestly that is how it felt in Bournemouth yesterday as we waited in the hall for the In-Vince-ible Tour to begin. Then, finally, the lights lowered and the lectern began to glow a rancid shade of mustard.

"Now settle down and shush," chided Lynne Featherstone, an MP and one of the tour's adoring fans known as the Vincettes. "For a soothsayer cometh."

The crowd went: "Ahhh" and Lynn lowered her voice even further: "For he spake of a debt bubble that would burst and it came to pass." Cue laughter.

"And he spake of having to nationalise Northern Rock and it came to pass. And he likened the Prime Minister to Mr Bean and it came to pass." At the words "Mr Bean" the crowd went wild, clapping, laughing, cheering.

Vince (he is ditching the last name for, like Bono, it is no longer necessary) bounded on stage to tumultuous adoration.

What a difference a year makes. The economist nerd who loved to give speeches backed by giant organograms has ditched the audiovisual aids and the nutty professor look. His suit was dun (not beige) and smart, the tie silk, the hair smooth. He was a storyteller, not a speaker, and he was word-perfect. Nick Clegg watched with goggle eyes the man many wish had his job.

Vince was almost glowing. He may yearn to be on Strictly Come Dancing but, actually, he has the X-factor. He is that rare thing: a politician who knows what he is talking about. For years he warned us of the dangers of debt and so has earned the right to say: "Those of us who warned of the dangers were initially treated as eccentric, then as scaremongers and prophets of doom. But we were right."

As he spoke (spake?), markets crashed and banks wobbled. Last year when the Lib Dems met, Northern Rock was collapsing. This year it is Lehman Brothers. "Some people say this is the curse of the Lib Dems," he noted drily.

There was a short, sharp attack on Gordon Brown. "Custom

dictates that I should make some jokes at his expense," he said to giggles. "But I have already done enough of that. ("No," cried the man behind me.) I am not a sadist. I have no wish to kick a twitching corpse." This got a big clap: the Lib Dems love a good corpse joke.

His attack on David Cameron and the Tories, whom he likened to one of those phoney American religious cults, was far more vicious. The Tories, he predicted, will wreak miracles. "Mr Osborne, like Mr Cameron, a graduate of Oxford's Bullingdon Theological College, will perform the miracles of the loaves and fishes on the public finances. The sick will be healed without additional health funding."

The Tories were now promising the "ultimate miracle": fairness. "There are, no doubt, people who believe that North Korea is a democracy," said Vince, "or that pigs can fly." But even those people were finding the Tory fairness pledge implausible.

When the In-Vince-ible Tour was over, there was an instant standing ovation. Then the star walked out, rock-star style, with little Nicky Clegg, looking rather like a groupie, scampering along behind him.

17 September

No one picks O-pick

My favourite day at the Lib-Dems is the one where nothing "important" is happening (some unkind people say this is every day, actually.) Keep in mind, as you read this, that outside, in the real world, everything was collapsing. But in Bournemouth…

Nick Clegg was scheduled to meet a bunch of vegetables

yesterday and, well, I felt I had to be there. But, as I tried to leave the Bournemouth conference centre to see the great kitchen encounter I ran into a strange man on a strange machine.

"Hello!" cried Lembit Opik (for it is the name of one of his favourite magazines), his goofy grin splitting across his long, thin face high above us, his body gyrating gently, his feet standing on a giant wheeled object.

"Are you OK?" I asked, for it is another magazine that he loves and, indeed, he has appeared on its cover with his Cheeky Girl fiancée Gabriela, whose big hit was Touch My Bum. Then I remembered that she had dumped him over the summer, which would explain why he is now desperately seeking publicity by hanging around on a weird machine that was related to a lawnmower.

"It's my Segway personal transporter," he cried, absolutely thrilled to be the centre of attention for three photographers. Lembit then explained, his voice a little too loud, that the Segway was illegal in Britain and he was campaigning to change that. "I am breaking the law just being here," he said. "But I don't care." He then went into what appeared to be a comedy routine. "I told the police it's Segways or Strangeways for me," he cried, allowing himself a little whoop at his own brilliance. "It's prison bars if I can't be behind handle-bars!"

Oh dear. We tried to escape but Lembit jumped off the machine, plastered with stickers saying "Ipik Opik" because he is running for Lib Dem president, and got another MP to try it out. "This is exactly the kind of out-of-the-box thinking that Nick Clegg wants us to do!" cried Lembit as we edged away, eager to make our date with the leader and his vegetables.

The idea was for Mr Clegg to join catering students at Bournemouth and Poole College. He may have had visions of making a soufflé but, as it turned out, it was vegetable-chopping day. The chef, a wonderfully bluff man called Dave Boland, had laid out onions, leeks, swede, celery and turnips on a gleaming tray next to a very large, very sharp knife.

Nick arrived wearing a white lab coat that made him look not like a chef but like an actor pretending to be a doctor in an afternoon soap opera. He surveyed the tray, his gaze lingering over the knife (Lib Dems know all about stabs in the back).

"Don't I relish this!" he cried.

No one laughed.

"That's a joke," he said.

He eyed the vegetables again. "I'd like to chop the easiest thing." Chef selected a stalk of celery. "You've given me the hardest vegetable!" squealed Nick. Chef proffered a giant tear-inducing onion. Nick backed away and began, gingerly, to chop the celery. My, I thought, watching him concentrate ultra hard on the thin green stalk, if he makes such a fuss about chopping vegetables how is he ever going to cut £20 billion out of the national budget?

We returned to the hall to find that, incredibly, Lembit was still there, slap bang in the middle of our path, chortling away on top of his illegal transporter. Now he was having his picture taken by random Lib Dems on their mobile phones. Out of the box?

How about out of this world?

23 September

Labouring a point in Manchester

The Labour Party met in Manchester with the kind of forced jollity that is necessary after a summer of splits and rebellions. For David Miliband, the leading contender for the big job, it all started to go wrong when he was photographed holding up a banana. Then he followed that up by slipping on one with this speech.

There was a turning point in David Miliband's speech, for him and for us. Davy was standing at the lectern, telling us how we'd saved swaths of Africa, when suddenly he turned to his right until his head was looking behind himself. Davy can do this easily for, like an owl, he has a swivel neck.

"Gordon!" he cried, looking at the figure slumped behind the long top table that sits to the side of the screaming pink stage. Gordon looked up at Dave and must have wished that he had never made this irritatingly perky man his Foreign Secretary. Dave trilled: "It is no exaggeration to say you have transformed the political debate about international development!"

Ouch. Now that's patronising. For once Gordon's rictus grin seemed appropriate. It's a bit like praising King Kong for all he's done for animal rights. The audience, crammed into the hall to hear the heir apparent, burst into applause. David looked extremely pleased, not with Gordon but with himself.

It wasn't the speech of a lifetime or even a lunchtime but it was better than last year when David had told us: "The world can be a scary place." Yes, it can be, David, and yesterday it got just a bit scarier for Gordon Brown. For it's official now: David Miliband wants to be PM. His speech yesterday wasn't so much a naked bid for power as a clothed one but I'm sure Gordo saw right through it.

Of course, that could be because Davy is so darned thin. And bendy. The man has a rubber face, that swivelling neck and incredibly long arms that seem to operate with an extension device. His eyebrows jump around like rabbits. The hand gestures are baroque: he has one that is like that "Here is the church, here is the steeple" hand game. Fascinatingly, his eyebrows at times co-ordinate with his hand gestures. It is easy to imagine him as being a cartoon first and a human second.

The speech was supposed to be about foreign affairs but it was really all about David and how he hates fatalism. Yes, "fatalism" was his buzz word. I don't wish to be fatalistic but fatalism may have been a fatal choice. It did not buzz so much as hum and, by the end, it was more an intermittent thrum, like a bee that has been trapped in a car too long and just occasionally breaks into an exhausted quasi-buzz.

David says he's not a fatalist because he has hope. "Now is not the time to turn back," he insisted though, as a head swiveller, he is always doing exactly that. Then he found his inner cheerleader: "These Tories are beatable! Let's say it! Let's say it! Let's say it!" The audience began to clap, possibly to make him stop his embarrassingly bad chanting. It didn't work. "Let's say it!" cried David. "These Tories are beatable. They are beatable, these Tories."

Oh dear. Now he told us he's not a fatalist because he believes in fairness. "An age of massive change needs leadership from a party dedicated to change," he said, as if Gordo didn't even exist. "We know those things. We know those things."

Do we? If so, why do we have to repeat them? Then, after one last shout ("Let us prove the fatalists wrong!") it was over and the hall arose for a 57-second standing ovation. Davy shook Gordon's hand (why?) and they both stood there, both grinning away as if they were in some awful toothpaste advert.

24 September

The Power of Love

Gordon had to give "the speech of a lifetime" but then his wife, the fragrant

Sarah, took the stage and the entire hall went all mushy.

It was Labour's "Sarah" moment. I knew that something was different when the comrades suddenly burst into wild spontaneous applause. It couldn't be for Gordon and, indeed, it was Sarah who stood before us — calm, tranquil, beautiful Sarah.

The audience swooned. She said something gracious. The words drifted by on a cloud of scent. She told us how wonderful that other Brown, you know, the PM, was. "I am so proud that every day I see him motivated to work for the best interests of people all around the country," she said softly, proudly, steadfastly, lovingly.

We gawped. This was better than Mills & Boon and Barbara Cartland rolled into one. Sarah was standing by her man. Indeed she was standing up before us for him. Now she fixed her steady eyes on us, her hair swinging gently around her face. "My husband, your Prime Minister, the leader of the Labour Party ..." At this point she seemed to forget his name but then she remembered. "Gordon Brown!" He bounded in through the crowd as Your Love Keeps Lifting Me (Higher and Higher) blared out.

They kissed on the lips, a bouncy one. The audience clapped the kiss. Their love kept on lifting them higher. It was almost a shampoo advert. Now came another kiss. They stood before the audience, adoring lovebirds and suddenly not afraid to show it. I suspect I was not alone in hoping that their love would stop taking them higher soon. And so it was, for now the lovely and adored Sarah sat down. This was greeted with rapturous applause. But Sarah had given the speech of a lifetime and deserved it.

"You can see why I'm proud of Sarah," said Gordon, with

an almost goofy grin. "I'm very proud to be her husband." They glowed for a bit and then Gordon got down to the heavy-duty business of saving the world and his premiership. The speech was 53 minutes long and had one real joke (it was about Harry Potter, he made the same one a few days ago).

There was also a humorous aside: "I didn't come into politics to be a celebrity," he said, weird smile lurking, "or thinking I'd always be popular. Perhaps that's just as well." This led to a ripple of laughter and, inevitably, applause.

The comrades wanted to clap. Indeed they wanted to stand. They began with a few partial standing ovations and then some crouching ones. But as the words flowed — and they really did flow most of the time — the comrades began popping up, like random pieces of toast. It was by far the most well-received speech he has ever made.

The content was vintage Gordon. He wants this to be the "British century". He's creating the "Something for Something" Britain. He's invented something called the "New Settlement". I loved this for it reminded me of his "Progressive Consensus". Do you remember that? Now that's given way to the New Settlement. So what was it? The details were vague. It was about hard work. It was about fairness. And, oh yes, under the New Settlement the markets and the Government are the servants of the people. I stopped listening at that point. It seemed highly unlikely.

The speech was so much better for the fact that Sarah was looking on lovingly. Gordon's voice seemed softer. At times he almost choked up. Forget the New Settlement. This was the New Gordon, caring, giving, sharing, kissing. Then it was over and Sarah was again by his side, in her rightful place. Their love was lifting them higher, once again. The crowd went wild.

25 September
RIP Ruth Kelly

Ruth Kelly's resignation was briefed by Damian McBride (better known as McPoison, a man who was to become infamous in the coming year for his ghastly emails) at 3 am in the conference bar. We were beginning to suspect that Labour was, simply, out of control.

So farewell, then, Ruth Kelly. Her resignation speech was, as perhaps befits a transport secretary, as pedestrian as can be. I was surprised that a lollipop lady was not required to bring her on to the stage. Ruth had slipped on to the top table in the big dark hall in Manchester at 10 am, a few minutes late. But, as her Cabinet career had ended with a bizarre 3 am confirmation from Downing Street that the resignation rumours were true, it did not seem all that unreasonable.

The comrades viewed her through bleary eyes. Ruth had been given the biggest graveyard slot of all graveyard slots at conference: the first speech on the last day. This was a time that delegates normally devote to nursing hangovers with a little light dozing before waking up to mumble their way through the Red Flag. Now Ruth had ruined it all by running up the white flag.

Gordon joined her on the platform, giving her a fatherly shoulder hug (has he been on a kissing and hugging course?). Ruth smiled up at him, looking about eight. Her jacket, which went perfectly with the ghastly shocking pink background, was bought during her second personal makeover as a Cabinet minister. The makeover, unlike much else in her career, had been an astonishing success. She is the only Cabinet minister ever who has had a makeover and looked better afterwards.

She began, as perhaps had no other resignation speech in the history of resignation speeches, with the words: "Conference, it is a pleasure to close this debate on sustainable communities." No one clapped, not even her husband, watching from the front row, but Ruth is quite used to the sound of one hand clapping.

"I hope you will forgive me for departing from my text," she announced, although in the text I was reading as she said these words that is exactly what it said.

She told Gordon before the summer that she had wanted to go in the next reshuffle to spend more time with her family (with four children, she is the woman who put the labour back into Labour). For some time the Tories have been taunting her with rumours of how unhappy she was. She always denied this, looking deeply unhappy as she did so.

But yesterday she looked euphoric. I could almost see the bubble "I'm out of here!" over her head. If she was unhappy, she wasn't going to tell us now. She even described Gordon as a "towering" figure on the world stage. Gordo, who is now on his way to New York where he personally will save the global economy, nodded, although I think he would have preferred the word "colossus".

She summed up her career in four sentences. Not everybody can do that. It is hard to imagine what the fifth would say — although, as a member of the shadowy Catholic movement Opus Dei, she was the closest we ever got to breaking the Da Vinci code.

"I am leaving the stage today," she announced and, after what can only be described as a zombiefied standing ovation, she did exactly that. It all seemed most inconsequential. It was the resignation of a Cabinet minister, the death of a political career, but it had all the emotion of a cardboard box. There wasn't a wet eye in the house. As she slunk off the stage, I thought I heard her shout: "I'm free-e-e-e-e!"

29 September
The Great BoJo Show

The news this weekend was dominated by desperate attempts to rescue Bradford & Bingley amid intense fear and panic about the global economy. But in Birmingham, where the Tories were meeting, the mood was a little bit different.

Just before the great BoJo event in the conference hall in Birmingham, there was a kerfuffle in the crowd. The cameras swung round to film the audience and, following their lenses, I could see the object of their adoration. It was David Cameron, who had "slipped" into a seat to listen and was now watching himself being filmed, his preternaturally squeaky-clean face looking even more squeegeed than usual.

Boris Johnson got the full celebrity treatment, including that most coveted of things, a pre-speech film tribute, in which we saw Dave watching Boris win on election night. So now, in the hall, we had Dave watching Dave watching Boris. And soon, when Boris arrived, we had Boris watching Dave watching Boris. Sometimes at the Tories you feel as though you are in a PR masterclass and not at a political convention at all.

Boris shambled on, his jacket flapping like a tarp that has lost its moorings in an autumn gale. His navy-blue tie didn't match, his hair needed thatching. His appearance was met by an instant standing ovation — the four Tory boys in front of me jumped up to video him on their mobiles — and wolf whistles. Yes, wolf whistles. What is going on? I'm sure Dave, his smile now so fixed that I suspected Superglue, hated that.

"That's really an extremely fine reception," mumbled Boris. "Much more generous, I must say, than in 2006, when I was physically pelted with pork pies." Cue hysterical laughter. "Or last year, when my speaking style was criticised by no less an expert than Arnold Schwarzenegger." By the time he said Arnold they were guffawing.

The stand-up comic (also, of course, the most powerful Tory in the land) continued his schtick. "It was a low moment, my friends, to have my rhetorical skills denounced by a monosyllabic Austrian cyborg." Now they were howling. His next joke, about terminating Ken Livingstone, brought actual screams of laughter.

How they love him! The buffoon has grown up but not entirely. This was his most accomplished speech, but he still takes risks when he speaks, although he no longer allows things to descend into pure anarchy, and the crowd loves him for it.

He had already thanked Dave once (so now we had Dave watching Boris praising Dave) when suddenly he pounced. "I notice from reading the papers that it's no time for triumphalism," he noted drily, for this had been Dave's mantra for the past few weeks. Now Boris peered into the crowd, already giggling, until he spotted his leader. "Dave!" he cried, his arm going up in mad salute. "Can I call you Dave?" he cried. "Yes I can!" Now he added: "I hope you will allow me to remind you in a strictly non-triumphalist way of some of the things we have done in City Hall." Let the triumphalism begin! And so it did. Boris trotted out his achievements to date, flagged up more to come, attacked Labour, defended City bankers.

At the end there was an instant standing ovation, but even as the wolves whistled Boris slipped out and Dave, watching

Boris but Boris no longer watching Dave, slipped out, too. The Dave and Boris show was over, for now.

30 September

Cupboard bare for Joyless George

On the day that George Osborne spoke, Wall Street plunged 777 points and the FTSE went into freefall, endangering the proposed HBOS rescue by Lloyds. George gave a speech that was terrifyingly depressing until the very end when he went a little mad.

George Osborne makes a magnificent Mr Angry. He didn't shout or swear yesterday. Instead he stood there, stock still, coldly furious, eyes glowering, blood boiling. You get the feeling that he prepared for his speech by sticking pins into a specially made Gordon Brown voodoo doll. How he loves to hate the man, and it shows.

"We meet at a time of national anxiety," he began, voice full of doom, having been introduced by the sound of a thunderclap, "in the eye of a financial storm." He frowned and glared at us. Oops, I thought, a hard rain's a-gonna fall.

And it did. The speech was like a relentless downpour that was more down than pour. He used to be Boy George and now he's Joyless George. It was all rather Old Testament. As he railed against debt — government debt, business debt, family debt — I began to squirm and felt the desire to shred my credit card statements. I don't think I was the only one. At times the audience seemed too depressed to clap.

"Gordon Brown is spending money like there's no tomorrow," intoned George, eyes burning as he stuck in another pin. "Well, for him there may be no tomorrow." He almost smiled at that, but stopped himself. Indeed, whenever the shadow of a smile threatened to play on the corner of his lips, he acted quickly and, like a cold-hearted drill sergeant, forced those errant lips back into a grim little line. Gordon Brown may have a stick-on smile; Joyless George has a stick-on frown.

The Angry Dad look suits him. He'd worked hard to look uglier than ever before. He's put on a bit of weight: those chipmunk cheeks have potential to turn into jowls. He's had the opposite of Botox and had special lines put into his forehead. He's done with that pretty-boy stuff, for he's telling the truth and the truth is ugly.

"Gordon Brown will do anything to avoid telling this country the truth," he said, his normally squeaky voice now as true as a spirit level. "So as he won't, I will."

He paused. Doom filled the air.

"The cupboard is bare," George announced, and I knew how Old Mother Hubbard must have felt. "There is no more money. Tax revenues have collapsed. Unemployment costs are rising. Borrowing is out of control."

Then, at the very end, Joyless seemed to go mad. He was, he announced, an optimist. I almost laughed out loud. This was about as convincing as Eeyore on happy pills. Joyless began an extraordinary chant. "A hard road lies ahead of us," he cried, voice lifting, "but that hard road leads over the horizon." Oh no, I thought, he's going to sing. "Over the rainbow will be Britain," cried Joyless. Was this a Judy Garland impersonation? As if in answer, Joyless warbled: "Strong again! Prosperous again! Confident again! Proud again!" Stop, thought I.

But now Joyless was standing there, applause washing over him, his long-caged smile breaking free. It was quite disappointing to see.

2 October

Dave, the prime ministerial doll

It all felt almost ridiculously grand, this final day speech by David Cameron. But it did the trick. We were all starting to take him much more seriously.

It was the new Dave who appeared before us yesterday in Birmingham. It was as if, over the past few years, we've been seeing various prototypes — green Dave, cuddly Dave, walking Dave — but now the Dave experimental phase is over. Yesterday the final product stood before us as Prime Minister Dave.

I believe the Prime Minister Dave doll will be in the shops soon (for Christmas, at least). You will be able to get him with various props though not, obviously, his family (at least not yet). He will be sold, it is understood, with his own lectern. He's done with all that walking around stuff, trying to prove he's young and fit. Now that he's a grown-up, he's put away those childish things and got a lectern.

The Tories had sold out Birmingham Symphony Hall. They began queuing two hours beforehand. As they poured in, they filled every seat in the five-tier hall, transforming it into a huge Tory wedding cake. The cake cheered wildly when Dave, the conductor, the leader, the man with the lectern if not the baton, strode on to the stage, ostentatiously clutching a sheaf of papers. The message was clear. The new Dave is not afraid to have a written speech: he's no auto-cutie.

Nor is the new Dave afraid to be dull and long-winded. He spoke for 64 very long minutes. And, like all prime ministers, he thinks he's got to tell us about himself. This took the form of an almost bizarre personal testimony. "I'm a 41-year-old father of three who thinks that family is that most important thing there is. For me. For my country." Those truncated sentences are very Tony Blair: the new Dave loves them.

Dave has a new motto: "Go with your conviction, not calculation. The popular thing may look good for a while but the right thing will always be right." The right thing will always be right. What does it mean? It doesn't matter. Prime ministers say things like that. The right thing for Prime Minister Dave is to say things like the right thing will always be right. Rubbish but impressive rubbish. It proves that he's not a novice. Indeed, his whole speech was aimed at proving exactly that.

I lost track of time, but knew he was coming to the end when he told us he was an optimist. "We will come through. We always do. Because we are united! Because we have had the courage to change!" Dave beamed. He'd had the courage to change. Now he had a lectern. He had a speech. He had rubbish sentences and personal mottos. He had the answers. As he told us, bursting with pride: "I'm a man with a plan."

When it was over, the wedding cake rose as one and Bryan Ferry's Let's Stick Together came on. Soon Dave was indeed stuck together with his wife, Samantha. There was a lot of kissing and waving. Indeed, I understand that the Prime Minister Dave doll will be able to do both.

7 October

The "Whatever It Takes" strategy is unveiled

By the time Parliament (finally) returned, the world economy was collapsing and Peter Mandelson was back after Gordon's shock reshuffle on 3 October

It was the "Whatever it takes" statement from the "Whatever it takes" Government. So far what they seem to be taking, mostly, is our money. Yesterday Alistair Darling told us that he's decided to give £40 billion more of our cash to the banks. He didn't even raise one of his eyebrows when he said this. If you aren't talking trillions, it's all small change now.

Gordon Brown was there looking his former gloomy self. Sitting a few seats down from him was the thin, hunched figure of Pat McFadden, an anonymous type who has now been thrust into the limelight as Peter Mandelson's mouthpiece in the Commons. This makes him, by most reckoning, the Princeling of Darkness which, on a day like yesterday, seemed exactly the right shade.

Mr Darling did his best to sound bored to death with global Gotterdammerung. He began with a sort of "What I did on my hols" statement: threw £100 billion at the problem, merged a few banks, nationalised another. The whole incredible list was emitted in a tone of monotonal dullness. Apparently, the markets were monitoring his voice and stood ready to panic if even one syllable sounded interesting. It didn't.

George Osborne, the Shadow Chancellor, said that unity was paramount and, in the very next breath, attacked Gordon Brown for the "Age of Irresponsibility". Mr Brown glowered back.

At times of crisis, we all turn to Vince "the Invincible" Cable to tell us what is going on. He thinks that Mr Darling will almost surely have to guarantee all deposits. "In my own modest savings," he noted wryly, though I bet he's got an immodest amount stowed away, "some of it is in the Bank of Scotland and some of it is in the Royal Bank of Scotland, so I'm more than usually dependent on the Chancellor, the Prime Minister and the Chief Minister in Scotland not to let me down."

Many MPs, desperate to take part in global economic meltdown in any way they can, talked almost total rubbish. Liquefy this, guarantee that, capitalise it all. One MP begged Mr Darling to keep nationalisation uppermost in his mind. "Well, I have, in fact, nationalised two banks in the last year," noted Mr Darling, face dangerously mobile. "I never thought, ten years ago, I would be able to say that!"

It was a relief when the Rev Ian Paisley announced, in a voice of pure gravel, that he did not have any answers. "There are many beliefs in this house and my belief in God is well known. I trust that our whole nation will turn in repentance and cry for God for an intervention so that the calamity will not come on our children and on the babes in the cots."

Mr Darling, face totally blank, voice flatlining, noted: "I am not as well qualified as you to comment on whether or not divine intervention can help us or not." Whatever happened to whatever it takes? Surely, at this point, it couldn't hurt.

9 October
It's a Knock-Out! Gordo triumphs

This was the first Prime Minister's Questions of the year and it was Gordon's best. It was a rare moment when everything went right for the PM.

It has been almost two years since Tony Blair jabbed his finger at David Cameron during one of their clashes at the dispatch box and warned him never to underestimate the power of Gordon Brown. In the political boxing ring, Mr Blair noted,

Dave would always be the flyweight and Gordon the heavyweight. "However much you may dance around the ring," Mr Blair taunted, "at some point you will come within the reach of a big clunking fist. And, you know what, you will be out on your feet, carried out of the ring."

Well yesterday was that day. David Cameron was slaughtered at PMQs. If this surprised Mr Brown, it didn't show. He had been up most of the night, his face as rumpled as an unmade bed. Yet he was on top of his brief (saving our economy and, of course, the global financial system). He looked comfortable in his own skin for the first time in ages. Behind him, his backbenchers roared their delight, the Labour beast back with a vengeance.

Cameron, on the other hand, certainly was surprised. Even shocked perhaps. Over the past few months he's been feted, lauded, petted and praised. Maybe he began to believe his own hype. Certainly, he believed it was a grand gesture — a serious, mature, statesmanlike one — to come to the Commons in the spirit of unity. His only purpose was to offer Gordo a helping hand.

Big Gordo looked at that hand, so soft and manicured, so metrosexual and, well, Etonian, when compared with his own hard-bitten stubs, and he reached for it. "I am grateful for the Leader of the Opposition's support," he said. "I welcome it."

Behind him, Labour MPs were not so polite. They blame the Tories for leaks that have sent shares plunging like a barrel over Niagara Falls. Every time Dave spoke, they barracked and bayed.

"Novice!" they cried. The novice, though already unsteady on his feet, did not hit back. He redoubled his efforts to sound caring, though it was in vain. Dave asked about small businesses and Gordo whipped out a two-page single-spaced typed statement about how he was saving them. Dave asked about "indefensible" bonuses and Gordo embarked on an almost Olympian speech about "executive remuneration".

Dave danced some more, now trying to bash the banks. "No one wants banks to fail but also no one wants rewards for failure."

Labour MPs sneered. It was only now that Gordo, knowing this was the last question and Dave couldn't hit back, struck. "I do hear what you say about what you think about the irresponsibility of people in the City," he said, almost silky, "but I have to remind you what you said on the Andrew Marr show: 'What you won't hear from me this week is the sort of easy cheap lines beating up the market system, bashing financiers'."

Cue Labour pandemonium. It was an easy cheap line about easy cheap lines but they loved it. "More, more, more," they shouted, waving order papers. Old Labour men threw their heads back, mouths wide open and howling, eyes shut, bellies shaking like giant jellies. I hope it isn't shown on television before the watershed.

Gordon, now sitting down, looked almost shy. It's been a long time since they loved him so. Across from him, Dave's moon face was a picture — hurt, disbelief, anger all travelled through. The Great Clunking Fist had done its work. Dave was down. I almost expected someone to shout "Stretcher!"

10 October

The flower fadeth but others endureth...

Once a month the Commons discusses God for 10 whole minutes but, even then, they couldn't not mention Mandy ...

MPs, exhausted by the demands of Mammon, turned their

attentions to a higher power yesterday. By this I mean God, both the real one and the one known to us as Peter Mandelson, now apparently renamed Lord Guacamole. Yes, I know, Holy Moly! Or even Holy Mandy! But before all that, MPs found solace in the Bible.

In a few years the King James Bible will be 400 years old and MPs want a proper party. Ideally they'd like a choir of angels. Sir Stuart Bell — who speaks for God, or at least the Church Commissioners, in the chamber — agreed. Credit crunches may come and go, but the angels were already booked for the Abbey, November 16, 2011.

Tony Baldry, a Tory MP who, in his total roundness, reminds me of Humpty Dumpty, beamed. "That is good news! Perhaps during these troubled times it is just worth recalling one phrase from the King James Bible: that the grass withereth and the flower fadeth away but the word of the Lord endureth for ever."

MPs murmured: "Hear, hear!" It's been that kind of week.

This set Sir Stuart musing on how much he loves the old version. "I was very saddened personally when a particular phrase which said, 'He washed his hand in snow water' became 'He washed his hand in water'. I thought that was a most sad difference."

Sir Stuart, who wringeth his hands often, sat down. Now up poppeth David Taylor from the Labour benches. Surely the King James Bible owed much to William Tyndale's New Testament in 1526 and Thomas Cranmer's Book of Common Prayer in 1549. "Without these, English would not be today's predominant world language with its amazing vitality, splendour and versatility," he cried, demanding more government cash for the 2011 Bible bash. Sir Stuart agree-eth. He would ask the Chancellor (I'm sure Alistair Darling has nothing else on his mind.) Also he noted there were new texts on their way including a Green Bible. "So the strand that began in 1526 continues."

Wow. From King James to the Jolly Green Good Book. It was all too much for Sir Patrick Cormack. He spoke of the Green Bible witheringly but I was rather taken with a book which, presumably, would map Moses's carbon footprint and offer recycling tips from Job. (I discovered later that the Green Bible will have, yes, biblical tips on the environment.) Sir Stuart now began to recycle some of his thoughts. "If I may divert the house briefly. During the war, Mr Randolph Churchill's mouth could never be closed. In order to keep him quiet for a while, he was bet a couple of crates of brandy if he could read the Bible, the Authorised Version, from cover to cover. Even Randolph Churchill failed in that task."

Whereth was this going? Sir Stuart sat down, dreamily, as MPs turned their attention to that other God figure — Mandy. A Labour MP wanted to try to make Lord Mandy come to the Commons for his departmental questions. "He should make statements from the green benches and not the purple settees of GMTV!"

Sir Patrick offered another green thought. "Many of us," he said snarkily (not a King James word, I know, but a good one), "are entirely content that Lord Guacamole should answer in the other House!" This was followed by some rather unheavenly laughter. Here the debate endeth — for now.

14 October

The Baron of Fey and Coy is born

This sketch includes Mandy, Joanna Lumley and 42 days — three major ingredients in the dangerously heady cocktail of a year that lay ahead.

Mandy did not walk into the House of Lords so much as slide. He was preceded by Black Rod, whose calves were looking fetching in his best silk stockings, and a man dressed in a heraldic tabard that made him look like a playing card. Then, without warning, as if he had come in on casters, Mandy was there.

He looked uncommonly solemn, his thin lips set in a wavy line above the huge collar of floppy ermine (he was born to wear ermine). It was no surprise to find him slightly stooping, causing his red robes (he was born to wear scarlet) to hang unevenly. His mahogany hair had been parted with a ferocity that left a white streak of scalp that looked furrowed.

The Upper House was at its most beautiful for the event, its huge candelabras a-twinkle, its golden throne glittering. The red leather benches were fuller than usual, both because of this spectacle and the debate on 42-days detention that was to follow.

Up in the gallery sat a gaggle of Mandy fans who included Tessa Jowell and Anji Hunter, two Blairites there to see the ennoblement of a third. Beforehand, in the peers lobby, the air-kissing had been conducted to a highly competitive standard.

A man in a periwig unrolled a scroll from the Queen. "Greeting!" he exclaimed. Mandy's hooded eyes didn't flicker. The periwig announced that Peter Benjamin Mandelson was our "right trusty and learned beloved counsellor". No one laughed. She would "advance, create and proffer" on him the "state degree style dignity title and honour of Baron

Mandelson, of Foy in our County of Herefordshire and Hartlepool in our County of Durham".

It was a simple title for a simple man. The Baron's head drooped a little to one side, his hair not moving. I know that he is Baron Mandelson, of Foy et al, but, as he reached out a languid hand for the Bible, it all did seem rather fey. Or coy, even.

"I, Peter Lord Mandelson," he began, his voice clear as a bell. He ended the oath by saying, "so help me God". Poor God. I'm not sure He really wants to be dragged into this particular oath. Indeed I'm not sure that Mandy would ever need the assistance of the Almighty for he can now, surely, just look in the mirror.

As Mandy wended his way from the Chamber, his fan club scurried down for more air-kissing. The glamour deficit was immediately filled by the appearance of Joanna Lumley, actress and campaigner extraordinaire, in the gallery, to hear peers discuss the immigration rights of the Gurkhas. Mandy slid back in for a bit of the debate on 42 days. He reclined on the front bench, looking a bit like a tourist. I think he wanted someone to take his picture. It wasn't long before he slid out for, as Business Secretary, he always has business to do. And so peers proceeded, without further ado, to completely trash the Government's proposal on 42 days. Even Lord Mandy of Fey and Coy couldn't stop that.

23 October

Sarah to the rescue

After the debacle in the Glasgow East by-election in July, when the SNP triumphed with a 22.5 per cent swing against Labour, it was all up for grabs in Glenrothes, so much so that Labour had to resort to its fragrant new top secret weapon.

To Glenrothes, then, to see Sarah Brown's campaign in the by-election. It was her first time and the preparations were ultra top secret. Indeed it all felt a bit like an episode of Spooks when I finally got the call. At precisely 4 pm Sarah would be going "door to door" in Carden Castle Park in the village of Cardenden. I was to tell nobody. I was given the number of the meeting place (or "safe house", as I dubbed it).

I parked some way away and walked up a road that seemed, well, rather middle of the road. The semi-detached houses, set back from the pavement, were in various stages of pebbledashing. New, tatty, grey, beige, brown — but all pebble-dashed. I couldn't help but notice the many Labour posters stuck to windows, tied to drainpipes and, even, a caravan. Clearly Sarah would not be in enemy territory.

As I approached the safe house (brown pebbledash), something wasn't right. Behind it, on a corner, I spied a crowd, bristling with cameras and notebooks. Ah, I thought, so it was so top secret that the whole of Scotland knew. The press officer insisted that we must keep well back. "This isn't what I say," he said. "This is what the seven men with guns who protect her say."

The crowd was restless but then, at precisely 3.58 pm, we saw something moving down the street. It was amorphous — a giant blobby amoeba with fuzzy microphones and Labour placards stuck to it — and heading our way. Was it Sarah? Lenses zoomed in. "Yes," cried one hack, "she's wearing brown!"

The debate over the colour of her outfit raged, though, as her jacket was a greeny-grey and blended perfectly with the street. I would call it pebbledash. Now cameras were filming us as we watched Sarah's amoeba progress rather drunkenly down the street. "Newstastic!" cried a journalist as the blob gradually began to look human.

Sarah was in the front, hair swinging away, looking very middle of the road, not to say Middle England, in a demure denim skirt, jacket and green shirt with black suede boots. Of course we weren't allowed to hear her but, from my door-knocking afterwards, we didn't miss much. "She's very pleasant," everyone said. "She's very nice."

Nice. Pleasant. Quiet. "She listened," said another householder, whose pebbledash sported an unlit neon reindeer. "She's very beautiful," said Catherine McNulty, aged 77. "The television doesn't do her justice." Catherine, like everyone else Sarah spoke to, will be voting Labour. Why? Because everyone in their various families always had.

You would never know in this street that the SNP are favoured to win this by election but the visit was not a set-up in the classic sense. None of the nine households had been warned in advance. But I could see Labour canvassers running ahead of her, knocking on doors, finding the occupied Labour households, and then giving other Labour organisers the thumbs-up sign. "Hold them there!" they shouted. The occupants would come outside as if greeting long-lost family, and within minutes Sarah and some other guy (sorry, Lindsay Roy, the candidate) would arrive to make very pleasant chitchat.

The only madness occurred off-doorstep when Sarah would plunge through the now much larger amoeba that was shouting questions at her. Her eyes never connected with us, although she did speak — once. I record her words here for posterity: "I am very pleased to be supporting Lindsay Roy."

See, isn't that pleasant? Isn't that nice? It was, I believe, a total pebbledash triumph.

30 October

What would Keynes say?

As the government threw money at the banks, our leaders were throwing names at each other at a classic Prime Minister's Questions.

John Maynard Keynes was cremated and so he cannot, by definition, be turning in his grave. He doesn't even have an urn because his ashes were strewn over the Sussex Downs. But if he did have a grave, or an urn, he'd be twirling away, for PMQs was all about him yesterday — and not in a good way. Indeed, at one point I thought Gordon Brown was going to shout: "My Keynes is better than your Keynes!" Yes, it was that grown-up.

The Prime Minister, who counts Keynes, dead or alive, as among his closest advisers, continues to flourish as the world economy goes down the pan. Yesterday he was positively frisky when he popped into PMQs, a tiny interruption in his world tour. (Surely the words that presidents everywhere fear the most are: "Sir, I have Gordon Brown on the phone and he insists on talking to you.") David Cameron does not look frisky. He still looks slightly stunned at the turn of events.

Dave began by booming on about whether Gordon would admit that he had not abolished boom and bust. Gordo boomed back: "We have had the longest period of growth in the history of this country." This seemed a bit out of date to me but then I don't know Keynes.

They had a fight over the fiscal rules, with lots of shouting and the occasional "It's not fair" type of squeal. "You were the man who was going to end the Punch and Judy show," cried Gordo.

Dave, furious, shouted back: "You say you want us to listen. We've been listening for ten years about your fiscal rules. You have stood there and lectured us about the brilliance of your fiscal rules. Why won't you now admit they are dead?"

The Tory scream track was deafening, but it seemed only to inspire Gordon, who now whipped out a quote from Dave that appeared to back Gordon. "You said, 'Borrowing is inevitable and you have to allow that to happen. These automatic stabilisers, as Keynes calls them, those have to operate'!"

Perhaps it was the word "Keynes" that did it. Perhaps it was the automatic stabilisers which, for most of us until now, were things that belonged on bicycles. (I now find that Keynes got their first and that, in his multiplier model, they can be summed up as: multiplier = 1/(1-[MPC(1-T)-MPI]). Good to know.)

Dave, who is, remember, a keen cyclist, went ballistic. "You have been going round telling everyone you are the new John Maynard Keynes with your plan for a spending splurge. Are you planning a splurge?"

Gordon, positively glowing, for he has known that he was the new Keynes for ages, shouted back: "I thought — you were quoting Keynes! — I thought you said you supported Keynes and the automatic stabilisers!"

Dave took this personally. "You haven't got a plan!" he cried. "You just have a giant overdraft!" Gordo riposted: "The Conservative Party says borrowing is the wrong approach. I say it is right!"

Or, as I believe it can be translated: "My Keynes is better than your Keynes — so there!"

4 November

Where has the money gone? Who knows!

The Treasury Select Committee began its probe into the economic disaster, calling the most important players to hear their accounts. The session did not inspire confidence.

The three men sat, in a row, looking like a trio of naughty, if rather aged, schoolboys. They may, in reality, be the most powerful men in the land when it comes to the economy but, for their appearance before the Treasury committee, they had donned the careful blank faces of pupils caught red-handed. John McFall, the Labour committee chairman, effortlessly adopted the persona of the stern and humourless headmaster as he faced the guilty three: Alistair Darling, the Chancellor, Mervyn King, Governor of the Bank of England, and Whatshisname, the new guy at the Financial Services Authority. They did, actually, look furtive.

Beside Mr McFall was a stack of 5,000 e-mails with questions for the Guilty Three from the Great British Public. The trio gulped. Mr McFall read out the first question, from Ted W. "Where," he demanded, "has all the money gone?"

The Chancellor began to burble about global situations. I don't think Ted W. will be too impressed. The answer seemed to boil down to: "Somewhere else."

Michael Fallon, a Tory, demanded to know who was really responsible. "We have this impression of See No Blame, Hear No Blame and Take No Blame," he said. As he said this, See No Blame, Hear No Blame and Take No Blame didn't move a facial muscle. Had they been behind the bikesheds taking group Botox?

Mr Fallon fixed his gaze on Take No Blame (the Chancellor). Why didn't he say he was sorry. "I said to you," said Take No Blame, "that I accept responsibility for everything that I am responsible for." The other two looked impressed, for this was, as I'm sure you can see, a wonderfully blameless answer.

Now came a question for See No Blame, also known as Whatshisname of the FSA, or Lord Turner of Ecchinswell. Nigel B wanted to know why no one had foreseen the dangers posed by the alphabet soup of complex securities used by financial institutions.

See No Blame said he didn't see it like that. He said there were two kinds of alphabet soup. The first was made out of CDOs, ADCP, CDS and CDO squared. He wasn't sure what could have been done about this (take out the Cs, I thought, for a start). See No Blame said the second kind of alphabet soup was made of SIVs and that was something that perhaps should have been seen.

Well, why weren't they all seen? See No Blame looked almost transcendental. "Sometimes the wisdom of crowds is deeply unwise," he announced.

Now came a question for Hear No Blame (Mervyn King) about the £37 billion bank bailout. "Has the taxpayer been taken for a mug?" Hear No Blame wasn't having any of that. "No," he insisted, "this is an investment which I believe will pay off." And so the blame game went on, for, as you can see, it's nobody's fault.

5 November

A knotty problem in the Lords

In America, voters were electing the first black president. In the world, the financial meltdown continued. In Britain we were talking about ... excessive vegetation.

It was an historic day but, in the Lords, history is not made so much as lived and never more so than yesterday. Here they take the long view. Global recessions come and go, as do American presidents, but in the real world there are other things that vex eternal. So it was that yesterday peers considered one of the great epic battles of our time. I speak, of course, of our war against the national scourge that is Japanese knotweed.

What, demanded Baroness Sharples, her body swamped by a gigantic scarf of sky blue, was being done to kill this horrible plant?

Lord Hunt of Kings Heath (which is probably infected with the stuff) said that it would cost £1.56 billion to kill all the knotweed in Great Britain. We needed that money instead to buy banks (he may not have said that but everyone knew it) and so, now, the Government is on the lookout for a biological agent. A shiver ran through the beautiful chamber, for this place is no stranger to the world of espionage: in the past agents of all types have found a home on the red benches. Lady Sharples said she believed that such an agent had now been found: her name was Aphalara itadori and she was a type of psyllid.

Peers nodded sagely (now that's a good plant). They knew that psyllids, which are plant-jumping lice, are the Mata Haris of the photosynthetic world. "As Fallopia japonica can push its way up through concrete," said Lady Sharples, "this is a considerable problem." I couldn't help but notice that near her, on the Tory benches, sat Baroness Gardner of Parkes, surely the perfect person to be at a knotweed debate.

It seems that the agent, which I immediately codenamed Alpha, was indeed known to Lord Hunt. "I understand that this is a knotweed specialist whose juvenile nymph sucks the sap from the plant," he said, with such relish that it was almost worrying.

Peers sat forward. This was very Day of the Triffids. "This is an appalling plant," announced Lord Greaves, "which, because it only spreads vegetatively, is all one plant in effect biologically and is said to be the largest female clone in the world."

The words Largest Female Clone in the World resonated round the room and immediately gained capital letter status. I have rarely seen the upper chamber so totally happy as at this moment. Lord Hunt told us that it was illegal to plant or dump knotweed but some "cowboys" did exactly that and they must be punished.

But surely this was a job for Alpha? So where was the siren psyllid and why had the Government not hired her? Lord Hunt embarked on an epic explanation of the Invasive Non-Native Species Framework Strategy. It seems that before Alpha can be enlisted he has to produce a pestiary assessment, obtain derogation from European plant legislation and consult stakeholders. (My heart sank for, as most plants can be held up by stakes, this could be a very large group indeed.) As he read out his long list of bureaucratic excuses, peers slumped on the red benches, too dejected even to nap. Lord Hunt, his red spectacles matching the red benches perfectly, insisted that all was not lost. "I can assure you that we are not complacent," he trilled.

Outside, in the big bad world, the Largest Female Clone in the World was winning the battle, if not the war.

6 November

Gordon and Dave and their new best friend Barack

The true nature of our relationship with America, and its president, was laid bare.

Obama-rama. Obama-mania. Obama-drama. That, yesterday, was Prime Minister's Questions. Actually I'm surprised we still use that name. Yesterday it was more like Questions for the President-elect's New Best Friend. For that is who Gordon Brown is now and he can't quit talking about it. Indeed, at one point, Mr Brown seemed to intimate that American voters, in electing Mr Obama, had virtually elected him.

The fawning was so intense that I half expected Bambi to be watching from the public gallery. Everyone who was anyone (and many who are not) embraced the new American President-elect. But it was when a Sir Stuart Bell actually started to quote Martin Luther King that I wanted to roll up in a ball and pretend it wasn't happening.

Mr Brown began by saying that his new best friend had written a new chapter in history. "I know from talking to Senator Obama that he will be a true friend of Britain," he said smugly, for in this case Britain was him and he was Britain.

David Cameron had his own little gush. For the US to go from the horror of segregation to the election of his new best friend in 40 years was an "incredible transformation". "The US is a beacon of hope and opportunity and change."

Dave savoured the word "change" for he believes that, like his new best friend, he is the change. But Gordon thinks HE is the change. Labour MPs barracked Dave: we may not have a

Barack but at least we know how to barrack.

"I read that you sent a message to the President-elect," noted Dave, "presumably it wasn't, 'This is no time for a novice'."

Gordon was thrilled by this for it gave him a chance to crow: "What I said was serious times need serious people! Once again you've proved you're not serious!"

Dave gesticulated towards the Labour benches. "You've made your strategic choice. You killed change when you bottled that election and you buried change when you appointed Peter Mandelson ..."

Mr Brown, who is quite the comedian now that the economy is in meltdown, taunted back: "The only change that you represent is you change your minds every week!"

I wanted to cry "Stop! All change!" but there was no stopping them. Finally Gordon just exploded with this: "The reason the American people voted for change is that they want progressive policies. They voted for a fiscal stimulus, opposed by the Conservatives. They voted for a rising minimum wage, opposed by the Conservatives. They voted for regulation of pensions and mortgages, opposed by the Conservatives. They voted for tax credits, opposed by the Conservatives."

I had to shake myself. The American people did not vote for tax credits, they voted for Obama. Most wouldn't know a Conservative from an Oldsmobile.

12 November

Pipsqueak Dave v Global Gordo

Things were looking up for Labour: the November Populus Poll showed Labour just six points behind the Tories (as opposed to 15 in October).

Gordon Brown had recast himself as a global leader while Dave was running along to play catch-up.

The battle of the press conferences began at 8.30 am, which, for Westminster, is practically dawn. The timing was all rather childish. When David Cameron heard the day before that Gordon Brown was holding his press conference at 9.30 am, Dave decided to hold his at 8.30 am. Dave's motto is: anything Gordon can do, I can do better. The only problem? These days he can't.

Bacon butties and strong black coffee were provided by the Tories. This is the kind of thing normally reserved for elections. They had come up with a clunking new logo of three interconnected cogged wheels that said: Keep Britain Working. When I saw the logo — one of the worst ever — I almost felt sorry for them. They are trying too hard.

There were other immediate problems. Disastrously, Dave looked fresh as a daisy. He'll need to get some eye bags. No one believes someone who looks like Little Lord Fauntleroy can save us from recession. At least he was accompanied by George Osborne, who, post-Yachtgate, wears the grim face of a condemned man.

It used to be Gordon who tried too hard. No longer. Now it's Dave giving us wide-eyed earnest explanations about his wizard new tax cut for employers. It sounded very complicated. If Gordon was watching — and I'm not sure he would have time now that he is saving the world — he would have found it all very risible. For Dave's plan covered only Britain! Gordon would have found that claustrophobically provincial.

Clock ticking, we raced over to No 10 to see Gordon the Global Leader. He did not disappoint, for he is grander by the day. He looked terrible, for, of course, he'd been up all night, phoning world leaders in the run-up to this weekend's Bretton Woods II. If he weren't saving the economy, he'd be a phone pest.

"This is a key moment for the world," he announced, for Mr Brown is now the arbiter of all key moments in the world.

The self-love flowed like wine at a bacchanalia. I was disappointed he wasn't still wearing his white-tie outfit from the Lord Mayor's Banquet the night before. Do you remember when Gordon shunned white tie? Well, he loves it now. I have to say it's a worrying sign, for it reminds me of all those African dictators who always end up wearing something with epaulettes. Gordon thinks white tie gives him global gravitas though, in reality, he looks as though he's the captain of the Love Boat.

He didn't say much about Britain per se. Gordon can't think small any longer, for all monetary and fiscal policies must be global. He wants a global fiscal stimulus package and a total IMF reorganisation. He wants Doha and he wants it now. Plus there must be global transparency for all, including tax havens. He wants to create a super regulator in which "colleges of supervisors" will crisscross international borders, laying down the law to the banks. Do pigs fly? They do now.

"The G8 is too small," he explained. "It's got to be more than G8 or G13. That's why it's G20." I began to suspect that the G in G20 now stood for Gordon.

21 November

Woolas is ungagged

Phil Woolas, the motor mouth Immigration Minister, would become a key character in the annus horribilis. This is one of his first appearances before the indomitable ego that is Keith Vaz, head of the Home Affairs Select Committee.

Phil Woolas, the new Immigration Minister with special responsibility for putting his foot in it, came before MPs on the Home Affairs Select Committee yesterday, supposedly ungagged. I was pleased to see him, for I had been under the impression that Mr Woolas was being kept under office arrest. I couldn't see his leg, though, and I suspected that he had probably been tagged.

Keith Vaz, the pugnacious committee chairman, feared for his human rights. "Was there an attempt to gag you?" he demanded. "Did the Home Secretary prevent you from appearing on Question Time?"

"We took the decision that ..." Mr Woolas began.

"We?" cried Mr Vaz. "Meaning you and the Home Secretary?"

"We, meaning me and the Home Secretary and the Government," explained Mr Woolas. Mr Vaz chortled: "The whole Government was involved!"

"The whole Government was NOT involved," Mr Woolas said, denying what he'd said only seconds before, which must be a record, even for him. "We took a decision that it was better ..."

Mr Vaz pounced again. "So it was a collective gag!"

"It was NOT a gag and it was a collective decision."

The only thing that was clear, after this exchange, was that Mr Woolas had now been gagged on the subject of the gag. Mr Vaz tested the conditions of Mr Woolas's bail further by asking him about comments he'd made to *The Times* about how the Government would not allow the population to reach 70 million.

"So do you favour a numerical cap on immigration?" Mr Vaz asked. Mr Woolas said that he did not.

"Therefore the comments you made in *The Times* were misinterpreted?" Mr Vaz asked.

"I find it interesting that the debate about immigration and population are confused," Mr Woolas mused. "Fertility and death rates are a major variable of population."

Mr Vaz nodded briskly: "A cap is unenforceable, unless the Government is proposing to issue chastity belts to everybody in this country!"

Mr Woolas sat back. "Mr Chairman, we considered the electoral implication of that suggestion and we decided against it!" "That is one very good piece of news!" Mr Vaz exclaimed.

And so it went on. Denial followed denial. At times Mr Woolas became almost runic. When asked whether the economic nightmare would affect immigration levels, Mr Woolas announced: "That is what Donald Rumsfeld would call a known unknown."

There was a prolonged spat about whether Mr Woolas supported Gordon Brown's statement on British jobs for British workers. Mr Woolas said that he did and then repeated himself (his electronic tag may now have been zapping him).

"But how can you enforce this?" Mr Vaz demanded. "It's actually EU jobs for EU workers!"

"I think that is slightly unfair," Mr Woolas said.

Mr Vaz announced: "The statement is not worth making is it?" "It is very much worth making," Mr Woolas insisted.

"But you cannot enforce it, Minister!"

"I see no contradiction," Mr Woolas said as the electronic tag zapped away.

25 November
Santa Darling's Budget

The Budget is a huge parliamentary event, staged to the max, and this year Alistair Darling was throwing money around like he was printing it (which he wasn't — yet).

Alistair Darling cast himself as Santa Claus yesterday as he came before us, hair as white as the North Pole and clutching a swagbag of goodies. He dove in and threw fistfuls of cash in the air, a £20 billion blizzard of notes, a Christmas giveaway like none other. Everyone was getting some cash, whether they liked it or not. The elves had printed the stuff, Rudolph with his red old Labour nose was delivering it, and we would jolly well spend it. Santa was ordering us to spend, spend, spend.

He was a Santa of the people and a Santa of action. "This is only possible because I am acting," he said (but not very well, I thought). Still, he bulldozed on with his Santa Action Plan: slash VAT, tax the rich, give to the poor, threaten the banks. It was as if Robin Hood had got himself a red suit and a grotto and, high on Red Bull and John Maynard Keynes, had gone to town.

But giveaways, like anything, can get boring after a while, especially when Santa has a monotone. "But I want to do more," said Santa Darling, although, behind him, even the most loyal elf was looking a bit sleepy. Mr Darling tried to look joyous — his "ho-ho-ho" really is only "so-so-so" — but only managed to look like he'd eaten a dodgy prawn.

It is Santa's duty to be upbeat and nothing seemed to get

him down. One trillion in debt! Yahoo! It would be paid off soon enough. The good news is that our financial Armageddon is not going to be as bad as everyone else's. Ours is going to be "shorter and shallower". Rejoice, for we are the lucky ones.

The Tories glared at Santa Darling throughout. As he spoke — and the red ink seeped into the Commons green carpet — the Tory front bench whispered to one another. In the corner, behind the Speaker's chair, a Tory financial whiz-kid type named Brooks Newmark tapped his BlackBerry frantically and passed notes down to George Osborne, the Shadow Chancellor, who then scribbled amendments to his speech.

Mr Osborne arose to a roar. "The Chancellor has just announced the largest amount of borrowing ever undertaken by a British government in the entire history of this country," he cried. "To pay for it he has placed a huge unexploded tax bombshell timed to go off underneath the future economic recovery."

He pointed a long, crooked, Scrooge-like finger at Mr Darling. "Stability has gone out of the window. Prudence is dead," intoned George, who seemed to be playing Ebenezer Scrooge as some kind of beat poet. "Labour has done it again. Massive borrowing. Rising unemployment. Tax giveaways for Christmas paid for by tax rises for life!"

Santa Darling glared back. I could almost hear him thinking: "I always knew that Scrooge was a Tory! How dare he even set foot in my grotto!"

But not only was George in the grotto, he was trashing it. This was Mr Osborne's best ever performance. You could feel the excoriating fury, and his voice, so often squeaky, did not let him down. The cheers for Scrooge (what would Dickens say?)

were deafening as he sat down.

Santa Darling got up and was more emotional than I have ever seen him (he actually used a few hand gestures). "He did not even mention pensioners," Santa cried, but, even as he spoke, the stain of red debt spread over the carpet.

We were all, truly, seeing red.

26 November

Stringfellow bares all

As the world staggered from crisis to crisis, MPs at Westminster got to grips with the not-so-niceties of lap-dancing.

Don't get me wrong but I don't think I've ever seen Peter Stringfellow when he wasn't wearing a thong. But that was in the papers, of course, not in the flesh (so to speak). It was still a bit of a shock to see Mr Stringfellow wearing a pinstripe suit when he came to Westminster yesterday. Still, all else about him was as expected: the grey-blond hair that crept over the collar, the tinted shades, the aura of loucheness that clung to him like a starlet on a sugar-daddy's arm.

The Culture, Media and Sport Committee's session on lap-dancing had attracted an odd crowd. There was Mr Stringfellow, a former dancer named Nadine Stravonia de Montagnac, and a beautiful woman who went by the name of Solitaire. She gave me her card that showed her, head thrown to one side, dark hair cascading, in a dress split to the thigh and beyond. Did she have a last name? "I just go by Solitaire," she said sultrily with an enigmatic smile as if she was in a Bond movie or something.

First up was Nadine Stravonia de Montagnac (we never did get to the bottom of that name) and a woman from a group called Object who, not surprisingly, objected to just about everything. "We should call a spade a spade," said Nadine, who had a permanent pout about her face. She'd been a dancer of eight years and thought the clubs should be classified as "sex encounter establishments" and licensed as such.

The women were almost painfully earnest as they explained how the clubs were sexist and objectified women. "You don't need to be a feminist to say that," said the woman from Object as a roomful of men stared at her thinking, "Yes, you do". Solitaire, sitting in the middle of the packed audience, looked enigmatic.

Now it was Mr Stringfellow's turn. "I'm a bit deaf in the left!" he shouted. "I couldn't hear it all but I got the general gist. The ladies don't like lap dancing!" The ladies, now in the audience, grimaced.

"Lap-dancing!" shouted Mr Stringfellow who, with his caged energy and hair was reminding me of a celebrity wrestler. "Not a term I like. It's a derogatory term. My term is adult entertainment or, in my case, gentlemen's clubs."

He hates red tape. "I'm not a sex-encounter club and I don't want anyone coming in my club thinking they're going to get a sexual encounter! Sex encounter licences in the West End are £30,000 per licence. Are you going to stick that on me? I don't desire to be treated that way!"

Mr Stringfellow objected to the women who had objected and noted that Nadine said she had been a dancer. "With all respect," he said, "that must have been some time ago." There was a collective intake of breath. Nadine looked down.

The men, MPs and witnesses now had a chat about the purpose of lap-dancing clubs. "In our premises, they're not sexually stimulated," a man from the Lap Dancing Association insisted. The entire room looked elsewhere. Mr Stringfellow, who kept raising his hand to be called, interrupted: "Of course it's sexually stimulating! But so is a disco, so is a little girl with her knickers showing, so is David Beckham in Calvin Kleins."

So we were back to underwear. Somehow I knew we would be. Solitaire, who really should be an actress, looked serene.

10 December

Camlet: to be or not to be?

The Tories, knocked off balance by the economic crisis, and Gordon Brown's larger than life role, were starting to gain confidence again.

To the LSE, then, to see Dave relaunch his economic policy. As I walk there, I spot a queue of people waiting to buy returned tickets to see David Tennant in Hamlet. What dedication, I think: no one would ever queue like that — and in the morning too — to see one of our politicians. But then I get to the LSE and encounter another queue — to see David Cameron.

Sorry, Hamlet, but I've got to say it. To be or not to be? That really has been the question for Dave (surely, if Shakespeare were writing now, Hamlet would have to be shortened to Ham). He's had a bad credit crunch. The slings and arrows have hurt, his poll ratings are dropping as fast as interest rates. Something had to be done — and that something was this.

Handily, for me, his speech was all about tragedy. Indeed, to be honest, at times Dave made Ham look positively cheery. There were many mini-soliloquies on the tragedy of Gordon:

"*To have spent so much, have borrowed so much,*
"*Achieved so little ... have nothing to say*
"*No apology,* [AND] *no contrition*
"*For the past.*"

I could almost see Dave rattling round in that desolate castle.

Almost, but not quite. The whole doom and gloom thing just seems so un-Dave. Ever since his seminal "Let Sunshine Win the Day" speech in 2006, I have seen him as a shampoo-advert type of guy. Still, as Dave said yesterday, extraordinary times call for extraordinary measures. For Dave, the smile is over, the frown is all.

This, then, was his Frown Launch.

Dave's solemnity was taken very seriously by the hundreds of very serious students who had queued for hours the day before to get free tickets. Up in the balcony, behind a porthole window, the unlucky pressed their noses against the glass. Inside, mobile phone cameras clicked away like mad.

Dave's message was relentless.

Gordon's policy of getting out of debt by going into more debt was deeply flawed. "Monopoly money gets more respect," Dave intoned.

"They should be punished for their economic crimes." We are at a fork in the road.

Dave wants us to take the Dave Way which, he said, will lead us to a "post-bureaucratic age". (I'm not making this up.) Basically this means a smaller State. Dave says it's so bad that the Tories won't match Labour's newly pruned spending plans. When he said this, he frowned harder.

I began to wonder if he was suffering from SAD. Perhaps he should get a lightbox. Now Dave was talking in the same Presbyterian terms that Gordon used before he went all spendaholic.

"This Government is intoxicated with profligacy," he said. "The bill for its binges adds up by the minute." He demanded an election.

Otherwise, he feared for the future.

He warned the audience that they could be the "Lost Generation".

They will graduate having to pay off their own debts and ours too. If Dave isn't elected, "you will be paying Italian levels of debt". The word "Italian" brought an uneasy laugh. Dave frowned more.

Alas, poor Horlicks (as Ham almost said). It was a feel-bad speech for feel-bad times. Ham didn't know how good he had it.

11 December

Gordon revealed as saviour of world

When Gordon said he'd saved the world, it was a Freudian slip of the tongue. The Tories went berserk though Gordon, of course, didn't see what was so funny.

Have I got news for you. Yes, BREAKING NEWS, as they say on the rolling television channels, from Prime Minister's Questions. First, Gordon Brown, master of immodesty, has revealed what he thinks about himself. Gordon seems increasingly distracted these days and yesterday, as he scanned his briefing papers, he looked unprepared. This is not good. Tony Blair, on the day he left the Commons, said of PMQs: "From the first until the last I have never stopped fearing it. The tingling apprehension I felt at three minutes to 12 today I felt as much ten years ago." I don't think Gordon feels the same. He's an intellectual: they don't tingle, they just think about people who do.

Gordon arrived armed only with an unshakeable faith in himself. The Chief Whip, Nick Brown, who was chewing gum so energetically that I feared for his jaw, caters to this by encouraging obsequious questions. PMQs began with one that Gordon preened as he answered: "We led the way in recapitalising the banks. We led the way in arguing for fiscal expansion. We will be leading the way in the next few days."

The Prime Minister, who thinks it is normal to beat his breast like a silverback gorilla, looked pleased. David Cameron jumped up to note that, actually, the recapitalised banks won't lend money to real people. "Do you accept that, on those terms, your recapitalisation has failed?" he demanded.

Gordon hated that and began to boom: "We not only saved the world ..."

This brought screams of joy from the Tories. The PM looked irritated. A Mexican wave of hysteria was engulfing the Commons while Gordon Brown stood, as stony faced as a statue. The Cabinet was doing its best not to laugh. (I saw Jacqui Smith smiling: she will have to be culled.) He tried to recover. "Uh, saved the banks, ah, ah, saved the banks and led the way. We not only saved the banks ..."

At this the crowd was chanting "More! More!" The Speaker cried "Order!" Finally Gordon, who can seem quite fey, flounced: "The opposition may not LIKE the fact that we led the world in saving the banking system, but we did."

Dave crowed: "It's now on the record! He's so busy saving the world, he's forgotten about the businesses in the country he is supposed to be governing!" Cue more hysteria. I have to say MPs seem giddy, drunk on adrenaline, these days.

16 December

Gordon saves the world, Part Two

When Gordon goes global, he doesn't mess around. Here he returned from his travels to update us on how he was especially intent on rescuing Afghanistan.

The Man Who Saved the World popped into Britain to tell us about his weekend. He'd had a global mini-break, a 7,500-mile jaunt taking in Brussels, Afghanistan, Pakistan, India and, oh yes, England. Actually he didn't mention England. Too dull. Too rainy. Too many irritating bankers who won't lend. It's so much nicer to spend a weekend wearing a suit in a war zone.

He had on the same suit but looked much more frazzled in the Commons than he did on the front line. His pile of papers has taken on truly global proportions. He was obviously tired, because all of his careful speech coaching went out the window: he stuttered, ranted and bellowed. I see that Alky Aida — his special name for al-Qaeda — has made a return. It was a five-star weekend and all the stars belong to him. First stop Brussels, where he saved the euro economy with his new best friend Fiscal Stimulus. He speaks of this, like Alky Aida, as a physical being.

"The debate about Fiscal Stimulus is resolved," he announced to fake laughter from the Tories. David Cameron leant forward and barked, like a cartoon character.

Then Gordon told us how he is saving Afghanistan. The language he uses to talk about Afghanistan now mirrors that once used about Iraq. I looked over at the Tories to see if anyone was going to throw a shoe but the front bench all had on lace-ups. Perhaps loafers have been banned as entirely too tempting.

"Our goals in Afghanistan are clear," he announced and embarked on the kind of "to-do" list that only God should contemplate.

First we are "confronting terror at its source". Plus we are supporting democracy in every way. We are also training the Afghan Army and trying to fill in "empty spaces on the map" that shelter narco-terrorists. He made it sound like a colouring-in exercise. Plus he is sorting the Afghan economy and there's also infant mortality, girls going to school etc.

It was exhausting and MPs on both sides listened with faces of stone. It's all been such a success that he's sending 300 more troops.

You could see people thinking: "And how many more?" James Arbuthnot, the Tory chairman of the Defence Select Committee who makes Eeyore look like a ray of sunshine, was gloomy.

"As I listened to you, I found myself agreeing with you but not inspired or enthused. Is there anything you can do to inspire the country so that it actually starts believing with some enthusiasm about why we need to be in Afghanistan?"

Gordon tried — Alky Aida got another mention — but the short answer seemed to be no.

19 December

The 12 Days of Xcess

It is traditional to serve up some seasonal jeer (sorry, cheer) for the Christmas break.

It is the last day of the parliamentary term and so I bring you an updated version of the 12 Days of Christmas. As we are all Keynesians now, I've retitled it 'The 12 Days of Xcess'. So, here goes. On the first day of Xcess my true love gave to me:

— A Prudence in a pear-shaped tree. This may sound odd (you try rhyming something with partridge) but this was the year that Gordon ditched her for good.

— Two turn-turtle doves. It's tough work being a dove of

peace in the new world order. Yesterday Gordon Brown announced, not for the first time, that we are coming out of Iraq. The doves fear that what that means is that they'll get back to Heathrow only to turn straight round and fly off to Afghanistan.

— Three French Euro-hens. We are getting to the point where nothing sensible about Europe is ever said in the Commons but everyone, at least, still hates the French (though not Carla).

— Four Darling birds. Opinions vary on what kind of bird: the Tories say that they are vultures circling above, while Labour sees happy chickadees bringing news of an economic renewal. Or, of course, they could just be turkeys voting for Xcess.

— Five gold rings. This refers to the Olympic rings and the price of gold, which hit $1,000 an ounce in March. (The average price per ounce that Gordon Brown received when he sold our gold from 1999 to 2002 was $275.60.)

— Six geese a-laying. The Prime Minister has ordered them to start producing golden eggs, large ones, for the election.

— Seven yachts a-cruisin'. Will George Osborne ever recover from that Bullingdon Club photo? The Shadow Chancellor may be holidaying on land from now on.

— Eight banks a-milkin'. Whom are they milking? That would be us, at least at the moment.

— Nine votes a-dancing. They belonged to the DUP and they saved Gordon Brown on the vote on 42 days' detention in June, a policy that has since been dropped.

— Ten lords a-leaping. Why? To please Lord Mandy, of course, a man whom, we now know, was born to wear ermine.

— Eleven polls a-plunging. For the Tories that is. (The December Populus poll has them leading by only four points compared to 16 at the end of the summer). It seems that the worse it gets, the more we love Gordon. But surely it can't last…

— Twelve whips a-whipping. Nick Brown and his whip-ettes have instilled new discipline in Labour ranks. Rebels will be thinking twice now.

So farewell, then, politics 2008. As Gordon would say: Merry Excess to all!

— ENDS AUTUMN —

THE WIFE [illegible]
MUCH MORE LIKE [illegible]

[illegible]

8. Westminster, the [illegible]
economic calamity [illegible]
anger [illegible] everyone seemed to [illegible]
he was angry. [illegible]
MPs claimed that [illegible]
Well, they [illegible]
politicians and [illegible]
blame game [illegible]
blamed America [illegible]
the country [illegible]
national [illegible]
action being [illegible]
hate [illegible]
were racing [illegible]
with a bucket [illegible]
but, as it turned [illegible]
it is now that [illegible]
some of those [illegible]
himself. In the [illegible]
boasting [illegible]
praising himself [illegible]
the subject of [illegible]

THE WINTER OF MUCH MORE DISCONTENT

At Westminster, the shock of an autumn of economic calamity turned into a winter of white-hot anger. Everyone claimed to be furious. Gordon said he was angry. Dave showed us that he was angry. MPs shouted that they were too. And the public? Well, they were beyond furious with bankers, politicians and just about anybody in a suit. The blame game was beginning in earnest now. Gordon blamed America. Dave blamed Gordon. Everyone in the country blamed Fred the Shred, our new national hate figure. (Actually, having seen him in action before MPs [see 11 February], he was quite hate-able.) The entire winter felt as if politicians were racing from one fire to another, armed only with a bucket or two of what we thought was water but, as it turned out, were empty anyway. But, also, it is now that Dave began to turn it round, setting off some of those landmines that Gordon had set for himself in the autumn with all his bragging and boasting. And the Prime Minister? He was too busy praising himself to notice. And, in the background, the subject of MPs expenses began to fizz.

6 January

The Year of Angry Dave

David Cameron must have made a New Year's Resolution that went something like this: "Get out there and own the political year". He certainly owned this day.

New year, new Dave. The man was bursting with a frantic and almost hysterical energy yesterday as he marked the beginning of 2009 with a Dave blitz. Perhaps he felt media-deprived over the holiday period. Perhaps Gordon Brown's gibe that the Tories are the "do nothing" party has hit home. But yesterday David Cameron did something and that was to get angry.

I woke up to Dave on the Today programme and he sounded like a man who'd been up since 4 am, working himself up into an absolute fury. He announced that Britain's "landscape" was "terrifying". Groggily I wondered what John Constable would make of that. What would Hay Wain Horror! actually look like?

"I feel like SHAKING the Prime Minister sometimes," he cried, "and saying: 'LOOK, what don't you get?'. It's a credit crunch! That's what needs to be addressed! Stop WASTING our money with cutting VAT. So get with the programme!"

Get with the programme? How about get off the programme? I didn't like the image of Dave shaking Gordon (all those flapping jowls, very dangerous to passers-by). I yearned for the 8 am pips followed by all that soothing news from Gaza. But no, Dave continued to foam (I do hope he's had his rabies vaccine) about the VAT cut. "The Government might as well have gone out and BURNT the money. It was a CRIMINAL waste of money!"

At the word "CRIMINAL" I left the room. There is only so much Unhappy New Year talk you can take before breakfast — Captain Crunch and the credit crunch just don't mix — but I suspect we will get used to this in 2009. It's going to be a politics-from-dawn-to-dusk type of year. Sure enough, at lunch yesterday, Dave called us to hear a speech at St Stephen's Club in Westminster. He was still foaming.

Dave walked in with the Shadow Chancellor, George Osborne. Both looked pasty. The Tories must have a "no tan" edict. Everyone must look as if they only have enough money to spend their holidays freezing to death in Britain. Dave was wearing a brown suede coat that shouted "Oxfordshire country walks".

He spoke from a lectern plastered with the Tories' new slogan: Now For Change. I wondered what it could mean. Surely that should be Change For Now. Or, even, For Now Change. Or, perhaps, Have Any Change Now?

Dave strode forward. "Happy New Year!" he said. "I am reliably informed this is the most depressing day of the year. As my wife said this morning, only you could think you could cheer people up by making a speech."

Cheer people up? Is that what he's trying to do? The speech was a cocktail of anger and hyperactivity. There are tax cuts for savers, cash for businesses, high-speed broadband in every home. My mind wandered. I was deep into devising anagrams of "Now for Change" when Dave suddenly announced he had a vision.

"It's an economy where government and its citizens live within their means, save for a rainy day, waste not and want not," he said. It's all about something called "ethical capitalism". Hmmm. It's going to be a very long year.

9 January
Gordon Meets "Real" People

Gordon Brown began the year by staging an "Away Day Cabinet" in Liverpool. He wanted to "meet the people" but not, of course, with anyone watching. I was banned from it all but managed to see this at least.

The sun rose at 8.26 am in Liverpool but Gordon Brown could not wait for something as tedious as that to start the day on his Great Regional Tour. So it was still dark when he made his way to the Liverpool Marina, where a police diver, dressed in a red dry suit, lowered himself into the inky water to check the Prime Minister's boat for limpet mines. Was this the coldest job in Britain? It was minus 1C.

The boat, with the unlikely name of Groove Armada, was a nippy little thing known as a sports cruiser. As the sun rose, the PM was feeling his way down the gangplank, holding the rail, hesitant in his city slicker shoes. His fellow sailors Andy Burnham, the Culture Secretary, and Beverly Hughes, the Children's Minister, held hands like children as they manoeuvred the slope. Then there was Phil Redmond, local hero and the man who created Brookside, who was acting as the PM's tour guide.

Thus the day dawned with three ministers in a boat, plus Phil (who, with shaggy grey hair and laconic ways, really is groovy), a PR and a bodyguard. The craft was guarded by two police boats (one with diver) and accompanied by a press boat with a PR and photographers (but not me, as I was banned).

The press boat PR was in constant contact with the PM's boat PR. "He needs to look this way," came the command.

Within seconds the PM was looking that way. Mr Brown seemed almost unnaturally buoyant. It really is true that the worse it gets, the better he looks. Yesterday, tootling by the Liverpool docks, the economy in tatters, with interest rates as low as the temperature, Mr Brown looked as happy as a sandboy.

As the PM cruised, on land at Albert Dock, his press team were fussing over his arrival. I'm not sure why. There were no crowds. Indeed, there were no "real people" at all unless you count the eight "youth champions" brought there to meet him. For reasons unknown, the man from the No 10 press office had brought along three small barriers with blue velvet ropes, which he erected in a random corner of pavement. "I think that's your pen," commented a woman to me. This turned out to be true.

The PM, back on land, his breath condensing into cloud puffs in the crystalline air, bombarded the youth champions with bonhomie.

"What do you want to be when you grow up?" he boomed. A small boy squeaked something that I couldn't hear from the pen. "A musician!" cried the PM, emitting a deep belly chuckle.

Now Gordon trotted off, treading through salt and mud, to tour a new museum (I'd like to tell you about it but I was banned). On the way back he stopped by to observe a large sculpture called an orrery, which is a giant model of the universe. This seemed appropriate for the Man Who Saved the World.

As his entourage approached, the woman next to me squeaked with excitement. "Look!" she cried, mobile phone camera out, "There's Phil Redmond!" And indeed there he was, right next to that guy the Prime Minister.

Gordon headed off to his "public engagement" event with 200 carefully selected real people. I was banned from that, too, though I did watch some of it in the ITN van on a tiny screen flanked by another tiny screen showing footage from a zoo. So, as the PM spoke (it was all about global challenges), I was watching a sloth go up a tree. It was surreal but then, that is what passes for normal on the Great Regional Tour.

13 January

Postnatal Dave bounces back

The Tories continued their New Year fightback on the economy by launching a campaign that featured an enormous picture of Baby X, the idea being he was born into a life of debt because of that horrible man Gordon Brown. Subtle it wasn't.

David Cameron, who has always denied that he is publicity crazed, gave birth to a giant baby in public yesterday. He did this by having a type of political Caesarean in which the infant enters the world via an advertising campaign. In future, this type of birth procedure will be referred to as a Cameronean.

Mr Cameron gathered 200 of his closest friends at Lindley Hall, Westminster, to watch the miracle birth that took place on a special "birthing stage". The event was introduced (speeches are an essential part of a Cameronean) by "Uncle George", the Shadow Chancellor, who has been at Mr Cameron's side throughout his pregnancy.

The event was full of doom and gloom. The Conservative Party, which denies that it is using the child for political purposes, had erected a giant "debt clock" next to the birthing stage. As the birth progressed, the numbers flashed before our eyes, recording a national debt that goes up by £2,500 a second. In this way we could see that the birth, which took 30 minutes, cost £4.5 million.

Uncle George said the birth had been painful. "I blame the

Labour Party," he scowled. We saw a film of the birth (it is essential in a Cameronean procedure to show a film of the birth before it happens). In front of us loomed a baby the size of a double-decker bus lying under a huge white blanket that must have originally been crocheted for a whale. The baby looked adorable as it moved its giant silo-esque arms to the tinkling of a xylophone lullaby. Baby X began to drink from a car-sized teat on a baby bottle.

This will enrage breastfeeding campaigners but I, for one, was relieved not to be confronted with a breast the size of a bungalow. The film told us that the baby weighed 17,000 lb and was to be called Gordon Brown's Debt.

Then, suddenly, the film screen fell to the stage to reveal a giant baby on a giant poster. The crowd began to clap. Now Mr Cameron bounded up on stage, looking a trifle wan. Still, I marvelled. Even that Justice Minister in France, Rachida Dati, took five days to return after her Caesarean. But here was Mr Cameron appearing only seconds after his Cameronean. Truly, this was a miracle procedure.

"I am standing in front of a poster of a beautiful baby boy — one of the most precious things in the world," announced Dave. I thought, for a moment, he might cry.

Dave explained that the baby didn't weigh 17,000 lb but owed £17,000 at birth. He thinks Gordon Brown's Debt is a great name. I felt sorry for newborn Master Debt. Just imagine having to explain that your whole life.

14 January

God v Mammon: guess who is winning?

When the government lifted the ban on short selling, the Archbishop of

York was not amused, setting the stage for a biblical clash in the House of Lords.

To the Lords, then, to see the Archbishop of York take on the Government over lifting the ban on short-selling. Surely no novelist could have created a more perfect setting for this clash between God and Mammon. The Lord may move in mysterious ways but so, too, does the Lords. The Archbishop sat in what I like to think of as the "God seats", beneath a huge candelabra. Behind him was a backing trio of bishops.

The Most Rev Dr John Sentamu is a mountainous man, much too large for the red benches, and yesterday his white robes spilt around him like an overflowing bath. Not many men can carry off an outfit with frilly cuffs, but on him, it's fine.

Lord Myners, the smoothy-chops new Treasury minister, stood at the dispatch box, feet splayed like a penguin. He wore grey and, indeed, was grey, but then Mammon never aspired to Beauty. He explained that the new disclosure rules on short-selling bank shares will reduce the potential for market abuse.

The Archbishop arose, gold pinkie ring glinting, and asked if Lord Myners was "absolutely certain" about that.

Lord Myners, who, like all City types, is probably not absolutely certain of very much these days except his own name, kept a poker face.

The Archbishop raised the stakes. Short-selling was all about rumour, he noted, asking: Had rumours ceased? "How come Belgium, France, Switzerland and Germany have extended the ban?" he demanded in a voice of honeyed thunder.

Lord Myners emitted a strange little gush. "The Most Rev Primate has waxed lyrical on this subject," he noted, citing a previous speech. "I recommend it to all who are seeking amusing anecdotes." Oh dear. I don't think archbishops want to be known primarily for amusing anecdotes. The Most Rev Primate observed the grey man coolly. It was like Moses confronting a mouse.

Now Lord Newby, a Lib-Dem who is married to a vicar came over all holier than thou (though not, obviously, holier than you know who). He said that, on the day the ban was lifted, a leading hedge fund manager had cried: 'Hallelujah! This should allow people to return to some sort of normality!'"

Lord Newby found this disgusting. "It's that kind of normality that brought the banking sector to its knees and the country, quite frankly, has had enough of it!"

At this, the Mountain that was Archbishop indicated his agreement.

Lord Myners refused to offer an opinion on this good versus evil world. Instead he offered this (appropriately grey) view: "The hedge fund community is wide and diverse and the taxonomy is complex of that particular sector."

The taxonomy is complex? Wow. I had underestimated Lord Myners.

Now he was thrown a lifeline by Labour's Lord McIntosh who, it must be noted, is also an honorary associate of the National Secular Society. "Are you aware whether the Church of England has been selling short?" asked Lord McIntosh mischievously.

Lord Myners, too grey to even twinkle, noted equally mischievously that the Church, while itself not directly involved in short selling, did engage in stock lending that could support the trading of short-selling transactions.

Touché. I have to say that I think it was a draw between Moses and the Mouse.

15 January

Mandy the puppet-master

All of the economic themes of the year surfaced in this Prime Minister's Questions' clash, though, at the time, all of Westminster was more interested in Tory Ken Clarke's come-back.

Lord Mandelson slid into the gallery in the Commons to watch PMQs, fresh from a morning of intense media activity. As of yesterday, there is no doubt that Peter Mandelson is the Deputy Prime Minister in all but name. Indeed he may be more than that. Perhaps it is Gordon Brown who is the deputy now.

I would love, just once, to be able to see the chamber as Lord Mandelson does. The man who behaves as if he is always being observed looks down on Gordon Brown proudly, eyes never leaving the scene below. Is he the great puppeteer? As Mr Brown answered his first planted question — Labour's propaganda is now brazen — I definitely saw Mandy's hands start to twitch.

The PM is as subtle as a bus crash. He answered the question about the new wonderful brilliant (I wasn't kidding about the propaganda) business loan scheme by emitting a slogan: "This is real help for business." Then he added: "This is real help for small businesses." And then: "It is real help for businesses." And then: "It is real help for high-technology firms."

Help! Had the PM, just back from his awayday Cabinet in Liverpool, been inspired by the great Beatles song? If so then, like an original 45, he was now stuck. After two more "helps",

I looked over at Lord Mandelson. Did his hands move? The PM sat down with a jolt.

Dave jumped up. "Planted question," he announced in a voice full of cold. I waited for the verb. "Copied policy." Was this a haiku? Was Lord Mandelson controlling him as well? Certainly it seemed so. Dave was not as wily as he can be. His performance was all Punch and no Judy and, if he is going to beat Gordon, he needs a bit of both.

Gordo hammered away, obsessively repeating his themes. The recession started in America. Everyone in the Universe is copying him. The Tories are out of touch. "It is a do-nothing policy! That is the Conservative Party!" shouted Gordon.

The battle was as familiar as a marital spat that always follows the same pattern. Dave savaged the VAT cut, branding it an "expensive failure". Gordo flounced that, actually, a figure none other than Ken Clarke had endorsed it.

At the mention of Ken, the Labour backing chorus went into action. "Ken!" they cried as if Mr Clarke was their best friend. "Bring back Ken!" Mandy's lips (not to mention his hands) twitched. All of Westminster is obsessed with the Ken Clarke comeback story and Mandy is stoking it for all it is worth.

Why? The general explanation is that Mandy is backing Ken to return to the Shadow Cabinet because, actually, he doesn't want him back. Yes, I know. But in Westminster this sort of opaque shenanigans is normal.

Dave and Gordo kept on trading insults about who was the more isolated.

"The PM is completely isolated!" cried Dave.

The PM retorted: "You are totally on the wrong side of the argument. If you want to be outside the consensus about what needs to be done, let it be."

Let it be. I think the Beatles must really have made an impact on the PM (Hard Day's Night could be his theme song). I yearned for Dave to start to sing a lamentation on Dear Prudence. Instead he accused the PM of "running around like a headless chicken". The PM smiled his crazed grin. Help! Up in the gallery, Mandy, hands quiet now, smiled.

20 January

Captain Gordon on an unhappy Monday

A few days earlier, the pilot of a US Airways plane became a hero when he crashlanded on the Hudson River, saving 155 lives. But, in London, Captain Gordon wasn't saving much of anything as he launched his second bank rescue scheme.

The Prime Minister looked like death warmed up at his press conference. His eyebags were like little shelves, his brow furrowed, his voice like gravel. He kept saying "I am angry", and it was the only thing he said that we knew, absolutely, must be true.

It was supposed to be Happy Monday. Gordon Brown had called us in at 9 am to tell us the good news about the second phase of his bank rescue plan. But it didn't feel like a rescue. If our economy could be compared to a plane that hits a flock of birds, we are not floating on the Hudson, wearing life-jackets with boats heading our way. Instead it feels as if we are in the water — freezing, cold, confused, even as our pilot, one G. Brown, lectures us over the PA system about globalisation.

Yes, it really did feel that bad.

Journalists — cold and wet — filled less than a third of the pews at the snap press conference. We spoke to each other in hushed tones. I almost expected Mr Brown to begin by saying: "Dearly beloved ..."

Actually, in a way he did. For he began with a little hymn of praise to himself. It was a "dearly beloved me" type of speech. He has stopped the banks from collapsing and, behold, the world has copied him. He has stimulated the economy and, yes, almost every economy in the solar system (he's beyond global now) has followed suit. Now the Great Gordo wants the banks to lend and, lo, he expects the world to take his lead.

It's strange how the world is both following Mr Brown, and it's to blame for everything. Nothing is Mr Brown's fault and nothing is Britain's fault. Yesterday he blamed all our woes on the US sub-prime market and foreign banks. Even the current crisis in lending has nothing to do with our banks: British banks ARE lending just as much as they ever have, it's those rotten foreign ones that have stopped.

But surely our own banks had not been honest with him? "Yes I am angry at RBS," he said. But then he remembered that, actually, it wasn't RBS's fault really. It was all because RBS had acquired a Dutch bank (foreign) which had loads of sub-prime debt (foreign). Mr Brown was almost in nirvana (also foreign these days) as he told us this.

So why didn't he just go ahead and nationalise RBS? Mr Brown ignored this. Instead he had a little outburst: "Anger is not enough! Rhetoric is not enough! One has to deal with the problem."

But Captain Brown was supremely vague about how he was doing this. How much did this second bank rescue plan cost? Was it a blank cheque? "Quite the opposite!" he announced. "You would be completely misunderstanding the situation if, in any way, you are suggesting this is a blank cheque."

But, as we never got a figure, it seemed that it was. We are all freezing in a cold cold river, our captain lecturing us from above.

22 January:
O joy! Gordon's in an Obama swoon

The day after President Obama was sworn in as US President, our own Prime Minister seemed just a bit besotted.

The Prime Minister seems to have a bit of a crush on you know who. Yesterday, at Prime Minister's Questions, he couldn't stop saying his name. It was an Obamathon. Every time he said the magic word, the Prime Minister's grey and haggard face seemed to be infused with a hibiscus hue of happiness that we have never seen. At first it was OK. Gordo sent his best and praised Mr Obama (savouring each vowel) for saying that he would act urgently on the economy. Then, because he could, he said "Obama" again.

David Cameron, pathetically parochial, asked a question about Britain and the new bank rescue plan. Mr Brown trilled that Mr Obama (third mention) was going to follow that very rescue plan. "The one thing that President Obama did not say in his speech was, 'Fellow Americans, let's do nothing!'"

Mr Cameron, still marooned in boring old Blighty, asked why the rescue plan had been such a flop. Mr Brown patted Dave on the head and said that when markets fail, governments must act. "That is the lesson that President Obama said will be pursued in America!" he cried (fifth mention).

Dave, spoilsport that he is, refused to talk about Mr O. Instead, he noted that Gordo, in the first bank bailout, had spent £37 billion on bank shares which were now worth £17 billion. "Will you confirm that, as matters stand, the taxpayer has lost £20 billion?" Gordon would do no such thing. He taunted Davie-no-Mates, saying that he was isolated throughout the world (sub-text: Obama loves me more than you).

Dave asked again and the PM retorted that he didn't understand economics: "You should really grow up and face up to the big issues."

Yes, well, we could all see how grown up it all was.

Now playground bully Dennis Skinner stood up and pointed a long, crooked finger at the Opposition. "Those Tory fat cats and the banks can't blame the trade unions this time for the almighty mess this country is in," he growled, to howls of protest. As if answering a completely different point, Mr Brown said that global action was needed:

"I am pleased that President Obama and others want to see that."

Oh dear. Surely someone (Sarah?) should make him stop saying Obama's name. In the end, our lovestruck PM seemed to be chanting it like some sort of mantra. Still, perhaps at this very moment, as I type, Mr O is sitting in the Oval Office, trying to take his mind off quitting cigarettes by reciting the many achievements of Mr Brown.

"I want to see Gordo," he will cry, "for he has saved the world!" Or, on second thought, perhaps not.

23 January

MPs agonise about the eX-Factor

MPs used to love to debate their expenses, mainly to explain how poor they were. It came as a huge shock to them to learn that the High Court had ruled that they must reveal the details for the past four years. How, they cried, could this be done?

To watch MPs debate the publication of their expenses is painful. It is like watching Galápagos turtles try to waltz or whales attempt to wriggle into size 10 dresses.

They try. Oh how they try. They discuss, mither, moan, twitter, footle. They wring hands, feet, arms, toes. But, in the end, it is hard to see if they are ever going to get it.

Take receipts. MPs are in the most fearful hoo-ha about them. As you may remember, the battle to make MPs' receipts public had to go all the way to the High Court. In the end they lost and, since last summer, the photocopying elves at the Commons have been scanning 1.2 million pieces of paper.

Harriet Harman came to give MPs an update on the Great Receipt Collation Task, for the scanning is only the beginning. "The receipts then have to be redacted."

The word "redacted" echoed round the chamber. What did it mean? Harriet said it meant crossing bits out. This wasn't a cover-up, she trilled: "There is information on receipts which would not be right to be in the public domain."

To explain, Harriet gave a little example. An MP goes to buy a ream of paper (already this sounded fishy — do MPs buy their own paper?). "But they also might buy a Valentine's card." A Valentine's card? Oh please.

But Harriet was very taken with what, for her, was a rather racy tale. "They would, of course, be paying for it all themselves but it's obviously not right that the receipt that shows the purchase of one lurid Valentine card should be put into the public domain and yet the ream of paper should be in the public domain."

I felt like screaming. Harriet plodded on: "Therefore, things that members have paid for themselves have to have crossed out."

She now waved at Nick Harvey, a Liberal Democrat whose nickname might be Dullsville. Harriet had looked at all of Mr Harvey's "unredacted" receipts as an exercise (proof she really is a masochist). "We were able to see from his receipts where he shopped — a man of regular habits — where and how he paid; not information required for the public domain. We would also know intriguingly what shampoo and hair conditioner he buys." Everyone laughed, for Mr Harvey has very little hair to condition.

I cannot tell you how riveted MPs were by all of this. Harriet said that, after some thought, she'd decided to give MPs a month to check the post-redaction receipts before publication. She told us all of this was costing £2 million. "It is an expensive exercise," she said, failing to add not nearly as expensive as the £87 million claimed by MPs in expenses and allowances last year alone.

Now it was the turn of Hunky Dunky, as Alan Duncan, the new Shadow Leader is called. He had been flirting outrageously with Harriet all morning (and she with him). "I am very sad to learn that if I were to send you a Valentine's card it would not count as a proper parliamentary expense." This brought shouts, for Hunky Dunky is gay. He giggled. My conclusion? Turtles are never going to dance.

27 January

Not guilty, m'lords!

When the Sunday Times *claimed that certain peers had offered to change legislation in return for payment, the House of Lords met to fulminate over it all.*

It was a day when the men in the "cash for amendments"

scandal stood up in the House to name and not shame themselves. This is a manoeuvre, unique to the House of Lords (though bankers may adopt it soon), in which men apologise for doing something they say they did not do just in case they might have done it without knowing. Fellow Lords looked on in admiration.

The day began at 2.30 pm (already almost naptime) with a heavy dose of prayers. I could see why. A *Sunday Times* story had claimed that four peers had asked for as much as £120,000 to help to change a Bill on behalf of a business client.

If true, this could result in what is now the ultimate sanction in the Lords — being the subject of a debate. (Yes, it's that horrific.) It is the first time that I have seen Lord Strathclyde, rather rotund and a Tory Santa figure, not jolly. "This is a deeply shocking and depressing moment," he said. "This house has been mired in a grim torrent of criticism about a culture of sleaze."

I half expected the Leader of the Lords, the flame-haired Baroness Royall of Blaisdon, to protest. But, to her credit, she did not. Indeed Lady Royall — I like to think her name goes with the word "Casino" though I believe her real name is Janet — was remarkably forthright. Yes, she said, if true it was "deeply shocking". Punishments must be reviewed, justice swift.

Swift? In the Lords? Up popped a man with a bristly comedy moustache. It was Lord Snape, one of those named in the article, a former railway signalman who was an MP for 27 years. "May I first of all apologise to your lordships for bringing this House, if I have done so, into disrepute." He wanted the chance to refute the claims.

"Hear! hear!" came the deep rumble of the Upper House.

"I note what you say," said Lady Royall crisply.

An aged man, with black Mr Magoo-type spectacles, struggled up. This was Baron Taylor of Blackburn, aged 79. "If I have done anything that has brought this House into disrepute, I most 'umbly apologise," he said (if he had a cap, he would have doffed it). He said that "within my own conscience" he had followed the rules over the 31 years that he had been a peer.

He sat down in silence, without any "hear, hears". Perhaps peers were remembering that, actually, Lord Taylor — whatever his conscience — had had to apologise last year for asking a question without stating his interest. On at least him, it seems, this jury of his peers is still out.

28 January

Hedge fund four at a hanging

In the drama that was the banking crisis, hedge fund managers were always spoken of as very close to the Devil himself. Here, then, was a chance to see them in the flesh.

They weren't selling postcards of the hanging, as Dylan almost said, but they should have been. The corridor outside the Treasury Select Committee was crammed as we waited for the hedge fund managers to appear. The MPs were huddled inside, knotting the noose. But where, I wondered, were the hedgies? A shadowy type (everything to do with hedgies is shadowy) pointed up the corridor. Ah, they were hiding! How sensible. Finally they emerged, eyes averted, an entourage of 30 scuttling behind.

The Fated Four sat in a row, ducks in a shooting gallery, albeit ducks wearing grey suits. They may be masters of the

Universe but, true to their hedgerow roots, they looked a bit weedy. One of them, Chris Hohn, was blinking as if he had never seen daylight. He looked more like a Mole of the Universe.

John McFall, the chairman, is styling himself as the Wyatt Earp of the credit crunch. Today he was out, pistols twirling, to clean up the hedgies. He demanded that the Fated Four tell us their asset worth which they did in turn:

— Paul Marshall said 5 million euros.

— Douglas Shaw noted that his company was worth $1.31 trillion in all: "Of which about $8 billion, only $8 billion, are hedge fund." Only $8 billion. It's the kind of thing that hedgies say.

— Chris Hohn, blinking, whispered $9.5 billion.

— Stephen Zimmerman (Bob Dylan's real surname by the way), said £2 billion.

All in all then, I was looking at an awful lot of money. But there are some things that money really cannot buy and the moment the hedgies started to talk I could see why they never talk. For they live in a bubble and seem to have no idea how hated they are. Indeed, incredibly, they see themselves as on the side of the angels.

"We've had some tumultuous times over the past year but I think that hedge fund managers probably worry more about their credit risks on banks than maybe banks do on their risks on hedge funds," said Mr Shaw (you'd think for $8 billion he could get someone to teach him how not to be so smug).

MPs asked about Paulson & Co, the hedge fund that made £270 million by "shorting" RBS shares over the past four months. Wasn't that a bad thing?

The hedgies saw it differently. Paulson was the victim of poor reporting. "This headline is somebody's attempt to estimate what Paulson made on the short position over that six-month period. They do not allow for any long positions he had," explained Mr Marshall as the entourage nodded and MPs looked on, eyes wide. Mr Marshall carried on oblivious. "You can extract one piece of information — on this particular period you made x profit — but that is a very very partial view. An aggregate view, we're not proud of it, is that the industry lost 18 per cent last year."

Ah. So the hedgies are victims?

Well the hedgies certainly think so. "The industry is not making vast fortunes at the expense of the public!" Mr Marshall insisted. "Blaming hedge funds is like blaming the passengers on a bus crash. The hedge funds are themselves suffering from the financial environment and some occasionally make profit and that is taken out of context!"

Talk about bus crashes. You don't need to organise a hanging when someone will do it for you, with their own words.

29 January

Gordon's global nightmare

By this time Gordon had lost whatever poll bounce he had gained in the autumn and his clashes with Dave at Prime Minister's Questions were becoming ill-tempered shrieking matches.

Most people, tuning into PMQs, would think that they had stumbled upon a mad house. Yesterday Gordon Brown accused the Tories of living in a dream world. "Ha!" barked the Tory Chief Whip, impersonating a wind machine as he exhaled all the air in his lungs at once. Other Tories, like jackals in the wild, joined in.

Dream world? I wish. Welcome to my nightmare. For one of my recurring bad dreams is not being able to get to my destination: I can't find the train, or the airport, the car or, sometimes, even the door of my own house. That is how it felt yesterday watching the Prime Minister try to duck questions on the recession. It began with Dave noting that we are in a deep recession. Would the Prime Minister finally agree that this was a bust? Gordon, lunging up, Mad Hatter stack of papers in hand, said: "Can I just quote him from the Institute for Fiscal Studies ..." The Tories went barking mad at this.

"They don't like it!" taunted the Prime Minister, who read out a quote saying that thanks to his marvellous policies the UK is going to avoid a deep and prolonged recession. Dave accused Gordon of "extraordinary complacency".

Gordon smiled his toothy grin that always pops up at the most serious moments: "This is a recession facing every country and continent in the world. Everybody except the Conservative Party agrees this is not a unique UK phenomenon."

Dave, digging in, shouted: "Let me ask him one more time! You didn't abolish boom and bust did you?" Argh! Would it ever end? "I've said this is a deep recession," said Gordon. Actually, I am not sure that I have ever heard him say that but Gordon made up for this (brief) slip by giving himself intense self-praise for every country is following him, the latest to do so was Canada (can it get any bigger than that?)

At one point the PM shouted at Dave: "Look, we can play his game of student politics as long as he wants to!"

Dave shouted back: "Only one of us was a student politician and he has never grown out of it!"

Student politics? We should be so lucky. This may even be sub-playground. I have seen pre-schoolers behave better.

What is strange is that, in the country, the recession has brought us together. As a people, we are hunkering down, trying to ride it out. At Westminster, though, the recession has driven politicians farther apart.

Certainly Dave and Gordo, now shrieking about debt figures, had no common ground. Dave said that we had the worst debt problem in the world. Gordon countered that our public debt was lower than that of America, France, Germany and Japan.

The Prime Minister scolded: "You shouldn't be going around the country saying the opposite of what is true."

I thought Dave would explode: "Those are the figures, that is truth!"

Gordon Brown, fury incarnate, charged the dispatch box. "He is NOT winning this argument. This is a global ..." The roar was deafening.

Gordon's mouth moved below. This is a global ... what? I think the word "nightmare" will do.

5 February

Watching the Pesto masterclass

MPs seemed in awe when they invited financial journalists, including the inimitable Robert Peston of the BBC, to testify.

The Treasury Select Committee clerk looked nervous as he surveyed the crowded corridor. Where were the witnesses? I pointed to a gaggle of hacks (sorry, distinguished financial journalists). "Yes, but where is Robert Peston?" Just then the dark and handsome BBC business editor appeared, a sea of people parting for him.

"He's here!" cried the clerk.

"This really is the Peston committee, isn't it?" noted one witness. "We really are reduced to third spear carrier on the left."

And the brutal truth is, yes, they were. (Well, OK, maybe Lionel Barber, Editor of the *Financial Times*, was first spear carrier on the left.) But this was the Peston show because Pesto, as he is called, has had a very, very good credit crunch. His stories have made him a star almost, it must be said, despite himself. For this is a man who, with his rambling intense way of speaking, can be excruciatingly to listen to.

I thought that, in person, he'd be more relaxed. I was wrong. Peston sat (in the middle, as befits the king), a picture of tension. He hunched forward, forehead scrunching, eyebrows up and down like a hotel toaster at breakfast. When asked a question, his entire face answered it. His delivery remains — there is no other word for it — appalling. There should be an L-plate attached to his mouth.

Did he ever want to delay a story? He hunched forward, face flying low. "Well. Um." There was a silence. "Um. I mean. It seems to me tha-a-at there are sort of two related issues here. I mean at the risk of sounding pompous and pretentious [shouts of 'Come on'] there is purpose in letting millions of people know what is going on with their bank and what is going on with their economy."

He rambled. The BBC had a "massive" verification procedure. "Huge" amount of thought went into broadcasts. At one point he announced: "I suppose the issue is counter-factual." Is it? I couldn't tell what the issue was — or the answer really.

Help! I was drowning here. I needed a Peston survival strategy. I began to see that normal listening patterns were futile. You need to go with the flow. I threw out any expectations of a full stop. Or sense. The key was to stay with him on this whitewater raft ride and expect to get a few mini-Niagaras.

Mr Peston was asked about his sources. Silence. Eyebrows zooming in like the Red Arrows. "Um. You will not be surprised that the one area where I, um, am uncomfortable is sourcing — of any source! Over the years I have benefited from, um, private conversations with members of this committee and, um, um, it is very unlikely that members would like me to divulge those sorts of chat!" I looked round at the MPs, thinking that, actually, they were absolutely dying to be so honoured.

The Pesto masterclass continued with occasional interruptions from the spear carriers. Why hadn't they warned us earlier about the credit crunch? "I don't wish to blow my own trumpet," announced Jeff Randall of Sky TV. The air was then filled with some really rather spectacular bugling.

Pesto allowed that he'd identified Northern Rock in 2003 as a bank whose business model was odd. "It was growing far too fast. For years I looked a bit of a plonker as the share price went up and up and up. I looked wrong. I looked an idiot." He seemed thrilled with this. I had to admire him: this sort of reverse self-bugling is hard to do.

But was he comfortable with the fact that he is now a market force? Silence. Eyebrows. Pursed lips. "I [PAUSE] am a journalist by vocation. Um. For 25 years, um, you know, all I've really done is thought about — how to get stories that are going to be of interest and relevance to, you know, readers and these days viewers. And. [SIGH] Um. Although I've noticed some of my stories have had an impact on, for example, share price. You can't [SIGH]. These things are in a sense peripheral ..."

I'll stop there. I think I've cracked it. I understood him perfectly. The MPs watched in awe.

10 February
Dave tries to smell the coffee

David Cameron knew that, in theory, he had to crack down on bankers. But what was becoming obvious was that he just wasn't sure, exactly, what that meant.

Dave is desperate to look tough on bankers but his heart may not be in it. "Bankers have got to have a wake-up-and-smell-the-coffee moment," he announced at his press conference, as if this were the worst possible thing ever.

I put down my Americano in a huff. Where does he get these clichés? Do bankers even drink something as generic as coffee? Surely what Dave meant to say was: "Wake up and smell the decaf triple non-fat espresso macchiato!" Also, who wants bankers to smell anything as nice as coffee? Surely they should wake up and smell the dog poo. Actually I read bankers are now so poor they are having to fire their dog-walkers. So maybe not dog poo. So what would be worse? My choice would be those awful little fir-tree air fresheners. Or bleach. Now there is a poverty smell. Yes, waking up to a burning noseful of bleach could do the trick.

Does Dave think about these things? I doubt it. He is a Tory and so the banking crisis is close to home. He keeps revealing this in tiny ways. Yesterday he told us that he is setting up an economic recovery committee with lots of people with titles. ("Between them they've got more titles than Joe Calzaghe"). One is Sir Brian Pitman. "I think he is one of the most respected bankers there is in Britain," Dave said without apparent irony. Yes, I thought, and who's the other one?

The Treasury review on bonuses is too late. "It's not so much they've shut the door after the horse has bolted," said Dave. "They've shut the door after the horse has won the 3.20 at Uttoxeter!" It seemed a posh update on stable doors. Perhaps this is how bankers speak. (Wake up and smell the horse manure at the 3.20 at Uttoxeter? Is that even remotely scary?)

Now Dave was on the moral high ground. "There is a simple point, particularly with those banks that the taxpayer effectively owns, which is an old concept, which is: he who does the paying does the saying. The Government owns this bank: it is able to make sure that good sense prevails." Good sense? Is Dave crazed? Wake up and smell the testosterone, Dave! If anyone had any sense, we wouldn't be in this situation.

So would the Tories now reject any donations made from bonus-rich bankers? Dave demurred: "It is a much better use of money to help the Conservative Party to win the election ... rather than buying a new Ferrari!"

A new Ferrari? Would anyone, even a narcoleptic bonus-swilling banker, dare to flash the cash in such a way these days? It seemed such an old-fashioned thing to say, the verbal equivalent of Dynasty shoulder pads. And it got worse. Dave wants to use "moral suasion" to convince bankers not to take bonuses. At first I thought he had forgotten the "per" but my dictionary tells me that this is a rare word for "persuasion". So forget the coffee. "Wake up," Dave will cry to bankers over the rev of the Ferrari at the 3.20 at Uttoxeter, "and smell the suasion!"

11 February
Bonfire of the vanities

Fred the Shred was one of the big four bankers who snuck in, heads down, apologies at the ready, to face MPs. So they said sorry but, you know, they didn't act it.

Make no mistake about it, this was a "Burn the Witches" event. The Treasury Select Committee has been working up to it with a few semi-lynchings (private equity bosses) and hangings (hedge fund managers). But this was the real deal — for surely fallen bankers are our modern-day witches — and MPs had spent the night gathering enough straw and twigs for four giant pyres. Now the hour was nigh and all they had to do was provide a light.

The mob waited in the corridor but the Guilty Four were nowhere to be seen, sequestered in a separate match-proof room. When the time came, the mob fell silent as they filed past. The words "burn baby burn" hung in the air, acrid and sulphurous. They did not look like Masters of the Universe as they skulked by for they had taken advice from Knights of the Dark Arts (PR execs) and, for this day only, they had turned themselves into mice.

"So is sorry the hardest word?" demanded John McFall, Labour MP and head witch-hunter, a long lit match in his finger tips.

The mice sat in a row, hunched forward, looking miserable. Their hands were folded before them (more Dark Arts advice). They wore sackcloth and ashes but I couldn't help but notice that their cufflinks, bought with evil bonus money no doubt, gleamed.

"There has been much talk of the S-word," said Lord Stevenson, a smoothie-chops who was chairman of HBOS. "We are profoundly and I think I would say unreservedly sorry at the turn of events." (The turn of events? That's one way of putting it.)

Sir Tom McKillop, white moustache quivering, formerly of RBS, made an "unreserved" apology. Next to him his former CEO, Fred the Shred (now transformed into Fred the Tread Carefully) squeaked that he too wanted to make a "profound and unqualified" apology. Finally Little Andy Hornby, the whiz-kid witch of HBOS, did a full-on grovel.

The match touched the straw. The witches said nothing was really their fault. Lord Stevenson told us about his "counter-cyclical" caution. Handy Andy explained how he had reduced the bank's reliance on property. So, he was asked, did he feel culpable? "Not personally culpable," he said. Whom did he blame? Why the collapse of the wholesale markets, of course.

I couldn't help but notice that the witches weren't burning. Indeed, they weren't even smouldering. Perhaps they had cast a spell by wrapping themselves in the word "sorry". Never have I seen sorry used in such a sorry way: these men said they were sorry but these were just words, empty as pie shells.

"You are in denial!" cried an MP, bellows in hand, fanning away.

The mice denied they were in denial. Sir Fred and Sir Tom explained that RBS had gone down, not because of them, but because of events in America that led to a crisis of confidence. Sir Fred, head down and voice low, kept talking as if he still worked at RBS. At one point he said: "I believe I've run the bank in a responsible way." I gasped: surely he would start to burn now but he didn't. Was he made of Teflon?

Then, at the very end, a glimmer of the old Fred. "It's just too simple if you want to blame it all on me," he squeaked. It had the ring of a phrase he's said a thousand times. He'll never burn. Forget Teflon. These guys are made of steel.

12 February

Hair-raising day over a prize scalp

At one point, Sir James Crosby had been one of Gordon Brown's favourite bankers. Then the country found out what had happened at HBOS and, suddenly, he had to go.

It was impossible to go to Prime Minister's Questions and not see Sir James Crosby's scalp sitting in the middle of the chamber. The banker who had gone from hero to zero in less than 24 hours had resigned at 11.34 am, just 26 minutes before PMQs began. It was all very suspicious. Until that news the Prime Minister had faced a stormy session defending Sir James. Now, with truly miraculous timing, that problem had been removed.

The scalp lay on the table, looking a bit sad in terms of actual hair. As a group bankers tend to be follicularly challenged. I'm afraid to say that in Sir James's case the scalp before us was as depleted as an HBOS balance sheet.

The first person to grab it and wave it round was the normally mild-mannered Labour backbencher Khalid Mahmood. It was most strange behaviour and I blame the whips. Mr Mahmood read out his clearly planted questions about how everyone hated bankers and Sir James in particular (I paraphrase) and wasn't it great that there would be an investigation into Sir James.

He threw the scalp to Gordon who, surprisingly agile for such a bulky man, made a perfect catch. He said it was right that Sir James — he gave the scalp a shake — had resigned as deputy chairman of the Financial Services Authority. Sir James would want to have the chance to defend himself (not to mention reattach his scalp).

Now Mr Cameron grabbed the scalp from the PM — it was rapidly shedding even more hair — and noted that Gordo had singled out Sir James to advise the Government and regulate the banks. "Do you accept that it was a serious error of judgment on your part to appoint him in the first place?" he asked.

The Prime Minister ignored the question. Dave draped the scalp on top of his own (thinning) hair and asked if Sir James, whom Gordon had knighted, was still one of the PM's advisers? I cannot remember the last time that Gordon actually answered a question at PMQs. It is a sign of how angry he must be that he now said: "He is no longer an economic adviser." "Ahhhhh!!!" cried Tory MPs.

This was too much for Gordo, who accused Dave of being trivial. Dave denied he was being trivial (though I did wish he'd take that scalp off his head) and shouted at Gordon: "Even the bankers have apologised — when is the Prime Minister going to? Won't you just admit that it was a misjudgement to appoint him?"

We were in deep Punch and Judy territory here. I do not think I am alone in wishing that the PM would adopt a change of tone and, for a second, I thought he might.

"Yesterday you heard the four leaders of the two major banks that were brought to the point of collapse apologising for what they have done," said Gordo. MPs watched, goggle-eyed. But Gordon had tricked us, for now he crowed: "If we had not stepped in to save the banks, I would have had to apologise for not taking the action that was necessary, but we took the right action!" Ah, yes, the right action. The Prime Minister now demanded that Dave apologise (don't ask) and ended by shouting: "Wrong! Wrong! Wrong!" Then the PM ran over and stole back the scalp.

13 February

Beware of the dog: Gordon's unleashed himself

The Prime Minister's marathon session before the Liaison Committee must have been exhausting for him. It certainly was for me and I was only trying to stay awake.

I learnt three things from watching Gordon Brown for two and a half hours. Our Prime Minister is right about everything (no exceptions). He truly believes he is saving the world. He is operating on a very, very short fuse.

My, but he was testy. One MP asked if he was becoming Crash Gordon not Flash Gordon. (Soon that may be Trash Gordon.) Whenever anyone criticised him he bared his teeth (it may have been a smile) and began to growl like one of those dangerous dogs that are banned but everyone still seems to own.

Take Peter Luff, a yappy Tory terrier type, who asked if the Government was suffering from "initiative-itis". There were many announcements, but little action.

Gordon growled. This was wrong. "A few days ago the same people were criticising us for not doing anything, now they are criticising us for having too many initiatives! What we have actually is a plan. The plan is very, very clear."

Mr Luff claimed that bits of the plan, for example banks lending, were not working. "I have to correct you. The schemes are working," insisted the PM.

Mr Luff disagreed and Mr Brown retorted: "Everything that we have been doing, with limited exceptions, is now being followed by other countries!"

Sir George Young, the bicycling baronet who, in the dog world, would surely be something elegant such as a red setter, dared to suggest that the VAT cut had not worked given our debt levels. Had Gordon ruled out going to the International Monetary Fund? Gordon dismissed this as an "absurdity" and "simply ridiculous".

Absurdity. Ridiculous. These are not normal words used by the Prime Minister. Now Tony Wright, the highly respected Labour MP who may, dare I say it, be wise, asked a gentle question. "When we have a catastrophe in this country we normally have a proper forensic inquiry to find out what the cause of it was and what the lessons are," he noted. "This is a big catastrophe. Don't we deserve an inquiry like that?"

Mr Brown hated that word "catastrophe" (not least because it had the word "cat" in it). "This is a set of global issues that are affecting every county. It started in America ..."

It was relentless. The only light moment came when Sir Patrick Cormack, Tory cocker spaniel, noted that President Obama had told America: "I screwed up." Wasn't that attractive in a leader?

"Absolutely!" cried Gordon, "and when I messed up on the 10 p tax rate, I apologised."

I remember that apology and it came grudgingly and after months of pain. I don't think Trash Gordon will make another one soon.

24 February

When in a hole, stop Digby-ing

Lord Jones of Birmingham, better known as Digby, seemed to have the answer to absolutely everything when he returned to testify about the recession.

If you could talk your way out of the recession then Lord Jones of Birmingham, better known as Digby, would be your man. From the moment I saw him in the corridor — big, bulky, dishevelled, looking like the personification of a fat cat — his mouth never stopped moving. When he ran out of people he knew to talk to, he approached us.

"I've been up since 4 am!" he said, "On the radio. Talking!" At this he started yabbering on about his new role at HSBC ("No bonus!"), then his rugby team, then the economy. He will talk about anything.

Indeed he may not have stopped talking since the autumn when he quit as Trade Minister. Then he was called "outspoken", Whitehall code for car crash waiting to happen.

Yesterday Digby did not disappoint in his appearance before the Business Select Committee. He proclaimed that 2009 would be the most difficult year since the Second World War. "I don't see any green shoots." But 2010 will be the year of "bottoming out". He was not, he proclaimed lustily, a three-year recession man.

Confidence is key. He blames our lack of confidence as a nation on "Robert Peston-itis", a reference to the BBC Business Editor whose mouth is also rarely closed (which may explain the animosity). Digby wants to see more good news. "We are NOT as a nation going to hell in a handbasket!" He then delivered an enthusiastic, not to say bombastic, lecture — he speaks in exclamation marks — on why we might be going, if not to Hell, then somewhere rather warm.

We need to "bang the drum". If Britain were a company, Digby would bang the drum and say: "This is going to be bloody. How do you address it? You trade your way out of it. Head down! Batten the hatches! Work hard! Deliver the goods!"

The Government is making mistakes. The first was the VAT cut. "There are better ways to spend £12 billion!" Plus it seemed unable to deliver on its various initiatives. "You stop people in the street and they say, 'I don't see it! I don't see it making a difference. Where is it?' The challenge for any democratic government of any colour is how do you get what you want to do [he banged the table like a drum] through?"

He despairs that the banks we own were not lending. "Somebody has got to be big and brave and say: 'You WILL!'" We all knew who that "someone" was: I suspect Gordon Brown would like to bang the drum at Digby, too.

Digby was full of bad news. Indeed, he was sounding Peston-esque. Digby warned the Government that it was in danger of blighting an entire generation with unemployment. He told us about Colin, a 19-year-old made redundant at Nissan. Why didn't the Government help Nissan and Colin with a plan that would have the company pay him for two days, the taxpayer for two and Colin forfeit the last day's pay? Digby would halve the number of civil servants. The Foreign Office is particularly worthy of a cull. As he banged on, I couldn't help but feel that when you're in a hole, you should stop Digby-ing. Except he never will.

26 February

The Chamber was hushed. The emotion intense

The Prime Minister, usually so flat-footed, came up with the perfect words to mark the death of Ivan Cameron, the Tory leader's six year old disabled son.

It felt far more like a church service than anything else as MPs filed in for what would have been PMQs, then sat in huddles, talking in hushed voices. For the first time I have ever seen, the chaplain who leads prayers in private every day was there. I recognised him only from his dog collar as he stood near the huge double doors, silent, holding a red, leather-bound Bible. The Prime Minister entered, walking heavily. He alone wore a black tie and everyone saw this and knew what it meant.

Perhaps it is because he is the son of a manse, perhaps it is because he too has lost a child, seven years ago now, but Gordon Brown yesterday managed to find exactly the right words and tone for this most unusual and sudden of Commons occasions.

He began by doing something that has become all too ordinary — listing the names of those who have died in Iraq and Afghanistan — but the three names hung especially long in the silence. Three other sons dead too young, three other families now grieving. "They shall not be forgotten," said Mr Brown.

He spoke — his voice ponderous and slow of pace — of the death of Ivan Cameron, aged 6, that morning. "I know that in an all too brief young life he brought joy to all those around him. I know also that for all the days of his life he was surrounded by his family's love." Tears pricked at this, though his voice was steady.

"Every child is precious and irreplaceable and the death of a child is an unbearable sorrow that no parent should ever have to endure. Politics can sometimes divide us but there is a common human bond that unites us in sympathy and compassion at times of trial and in support for each other at times of grief." Mr Brown sat down to a sombre "hear hear". It was impossible not to see the grief that radiated from those knotted shoulders.

Everyone looking saw how losing a child sets you apart, marks you, pierces through all. The two men who so often trade ferocious attacks at PMQs have more in common than is apparent.

William Hague, his sonorous voice especially welcome, was the perfect man for this difficult job. He thanked Mr Brown for the offer to suspend the normal exchanges at PMQs. "Ivan's six years of life were not easy ones. His parents lived with the knowledge for a long time that he could die young. But this has made their loss no less heartbreaking." Mr Hague passed on the Camerons' gratitude to NHS staff, both those who had helped their son that morning but also every day since his birth. "Ivan suffered much in his short life but he brought joy and love to those around him," said Mr Hague, "and as David himself has said in the past, for him and Samantha he will always be their beautiful boy."

The Chamber was hushed. The emotion intense. MPs listened as Vince Cable, standing in for Nick Clegg, absent after the birth of his third son, delivered a short tribute. At 12.06, the Speaker suspended the House until 12.30 as a mark of respect for Ivan, the first time such a thing has been done for a child.

Mr Brown, who normally rushes out, stood by himself behind the Speaker's Chair, waiting for Mr Hague. When he arrived, the Prime Minister put his hand on his back and they walked out together. Everyone else milled around, not knowing what to do.

27 February

MPs shred the Fred

In the wake of news breaking about Sir Fred Goodwin's enormous pension, MPs were beside themselves with fury. It was, truly, a toxic session.

It's official. In the Commons yesterday Fred the Shred became Fred the Shredded.

MPs, furious that his pension is even larger than theirs, were in full cry. By the end the man who once ran the Royal Bank of Scotland was reduced to a mass of paper spaghetti, a packing material even lowlier than bubblewrap.

"Disgraceful!" MPs shouted at every mention of his name.

Alistair Darling tried to join in though, as usual, it was hard to tell if he was angry or just twitching his eyebrow. Actually he may have welcomed the row. The Chancellor had come to tell us why we must give even more shed-loads (shred-loads?) to bail out RBS. Surely the Fred row would divert attention from that.

But it didn't quite work out like that. "Who exactly in the Government knew about this deal?" demanded George Osborne. "This obscene pension is unacceptable and the Government is on the hook: either they did know and failed to act, or they didn't know and failed to ask the right questions. It is a totally irresponsible use of taxpayer money."

George called on Sir Fred to do the right thing. Mr Darling, eyebrow salsa-ing, agreed: "It is beyond doubt that most people find it very hard to understand, given what has happened to RBS, that such an enormous pension can be paid from the age of 50." (No, Chancellor, we find it hard to believe that Fred the Shred, the epitome of failure, is getting any such pension at any age, ever.)

Mr Darling announced that he had known nothing about the details. "This agreement was not negotiated by the Government, nor was it approved by the Government, nor would it have been!" Andrew Mackay, a Tory whose orangeness is cause for concern, heckled the Chancellor, asking when he knew about the deal.

"Last week actually," gabbled Alistair. MPs gasped. (I took this to mean he hadn't known a thing until then. Later, however, it emerged Mr Darling only hadn't known the contractual details. Politicians are brilliant at thin-slicing the truth.)

The speech by Vince Cable, half-moon specs almost all the way down his nose, was a shred-fest. "We don't just have zombie banks. We have a zombie Government!" he declared. At the word "zombie" Mr Darling looked even more vacant than usual.

Vince said the Government had lost the plot. The toxic assets plan was a disgrace and, indeed, nothing more than fraud at the taxpayer's expense. Sir Fred should give up his pension. "This is public expenditure. This is a massive public spending increase, public wages, for which there is no justification whatever."

Next up was Dennis Skinner. The Beast of Bolsover agreed with the Tories (how that must have hurt). "I've got a novel suggestion. Instead of paying out these vast executive bonuses and Freddy Goodwin's massive £650,000 pension ..."

At this a Tory, no doubt envious, shouted "PER YEAR!"

The Beast suggested all such pay-outs should only be paid out when and if the toxic debt has been repaid (ie, never). "That's the proposal that we ought to put to these bankers and treat them with the contempt they deserve."

Toxic debt. Toxic bankers. Toxic day. Shreds of the very rich Sir Fred floated through the air. For now, Mr Darling remains in one piece.

3 March

Gordon takes time out for man-banter

Before Gordon Brown went to America to meet President Obama, there was just one thing he had to do: appear on talkSPORT radio. Obviously.

The Prime Minister launched his historic trip to America with a pre-tour interview on talkSPORT radio. Yes, for an hour, the P&T (Mike Parry and Andy Townsend) show became talkGORDON. It isn't often that we hear the PM quite so live and unplugged and, dare I say it, ever so slightly unhinged.

It began with a little man-banter.

Did Gordo catch the match? The Prime Minister had not (for he'd been at that pesky Euro-summit), so he'd had to watch the Man U v Spurs match "on tape" starting at 11 pm. "And so I saw the penalties this morning!" he said, laughing merrily. (And there I was thinking he'd be worrying about Fred the Shred's pension.)

Now P&T asked the big one. What about those Raith Rovers then? "Three-three on Saturday," said Gordo happily. "Three-three yeah!" cried P (or T). "All goals in the first half!" added Gordon.

As you can see, it was a tough interview but someone has to do it.

"Prime Minister, Gordon, thank you for letting us call you Gordon!" cried T (or P). Gordon rumbled even more happily at this and launched into a pre-trip chat about America. "What I want to talk about is the renewal of our relationship for new times," he said. "There is a progressive relationship to be built." What does it mean?

Then, suddenly, we were going live to Heathrow to talk to Russell, a small businessman worried about debt. "All the debt is blamed on the American sub-prime," Russell protested to the man who has done exactly that for the past year. But Gordon ducked that and instead explained that he was bailing out the banks for the likes of Russell. "I want the money flowing to YOU. I want the money to flow to YOU."

Russell asked about why his money was flowing to the banks. Gordon explained that we were not giving money to the banks, merely lending it. "It's not something for nothing. It is nothing for nothing. It's something for something."

Ah, yes, well that's clear then. Bernard came on from Yorkshire. "We need to see more police on the streets. Don't fob us off! We really do!"

Gordon insisted there were more police.

"Another thing!" cried Bernard. "No more fat cats! Sick of 'em! Get rid of 'em!"

P (or T) said, almost apologetically: "That, actually, is the attitude of a lot of people."

Gordo jumped in. "You know, I agree! Because, look, I didn't come into politics to defend the behaviour of the banks! I want to change the behaviour of the banks!"

So, asked T (or P), did Gordon have any little bit of optimism to offer? Any idea when things will get better? Gordon did indeed. We had a "great future". Reasons to be cheerful included fashion, film, music and design. Plus, he noted, we have "great pharmaceuticals" and "are leading the world in video games!"

Video games? That's the ray of sunshine? Well there's that and Raith Rovers I guess.

4 March

Making it up as you go, the Uckfee way

The two men appointed to represent British taxpayers in the banking crisis appeared before the Treasury Select Committee — and bombed.

It all began with the most tremendous hissy fit. Glen Moreno and John Kingman, the two men who have been appointed to represent taxpayers in the banking crisis, had just arrived. The Treasury Select Committee's chairman, John McFall, had asked them how many RBS staff received more than £100,000 in 2008.

"I don't have those figures," said John Kingman blithely.

Mr McFall, spluttering, asked again. Mr Kingman repeated himself. But, Mr McFall protested, the committee clerk had rung them last week to give notice of the question so they could get the figures. Mr Kingman looked not the least bit interested. "Scandalous!" cried one MP. "Disgraceful!" shouted another. "Is there any point in even going on!" huffed Mr McFall.

I know that Mr McFall was being precious but I have some sympathy.

Mr Moreno and Mr Kingman are the chairman and the chief executive of UK Financial Investments, a quango set up to oversee our considerable stake in the troubled banks. Surely they should be world experts on RBS pay and bonuses?

They make a bit of a comedy duo, actually. John Kingman, 39 and prematurely balding, is a posh, clever, not to say arrogant civil servant. Mr Moreno, in his sixties, is a lugubrious American with the folksy charm of an airline pilot, though, it must be said, I suspect he's no stranger to private jets.

At one point he explained how UKFI — which, unfortunately, is referred to as Uckfee — was a small quango: "The chief executive makes less than John Thain's chauffeur!" MPs looked blank. (The ex-Merrill Lynch boss's driver made $230,000 a year.)

I'm not sure at which point I realised that these two guys are making it up as they went along. Was it when Mr Kingman earnestly explained why Uckfee was paying bonuses itself? Was it when neither of the men knew their own running costs? Was it when the list of things they didn't know just grew and grew?

Indeed, when it came to Fred the Shred's pension, they knew only what they hadn't known. They defended the City Minister, Lord Myners, for he, too, didn't know what he wasn't told.

"I do think Fred should have walked," said Glen. "I think he's the kind of guy who would have said 'I'm leaving, goodbye!' The pension thing is just too complicated ..."

So, there you have it — the pension thing is just too complicated. But surely, MPs insisted, it was only common sense for Lord Myners to challenge a figure like £697,000 per year?

"I don't know if anything makes sense when you are trying to get rid of these guys and save the banking system," Mr Moreno noted laconically.

Do you see what I mean by making it up as they go along?

5 March

Little Miss Plod's 32 second triumph

As Labour's poll ratings faltered (the gap between the two main parties was 14 points again), there were rumours that Harriet Harman had her eye on the top job. With Gordon away in America, Harriet stood in for him at Prime Minister's Questions.

At one point yesterday William Hague egged on Harriet Harman in her Labour leadership campaign: "This could be your moment!" But it wasn't. It wasn't her day, her half-hour, her minute. Indeed, I can tell you exactly how much of PMQs belonged to Harriet and it was 32 seconds. Is that a moment? Get your stopwatch out.

The thing about Harriet is that she's deeply dogged. This is both her best and worst trait. If she were a character in the Little Miss books, she'd be Little Miss Plod. This was fine when she was on the fringes. Now that she is a potential leader, Labour MPs seem uneasy. For most of PMQs, I couldn't decide if they had been drugged or were asleep with their eyes open. It was like looking at a Catatonics Anonymous meeting.

Mr Hague, in contrast, sparkled like a jewelled pinkie ring. He began by asking why a series of government schemes to help the economy had not started. Harriet could not say. "When! When!" shouted Tory MPs at her.

"Why don't you step in?" urged Mr Hague. "When Chamberlain lost his party's confidence, Churchill stepped forward." At the word Churchill, there was hilarity. David Miliband, the Foreign Secretary, was unable to control his facial muscles. Nick Brown, the Chief Whip, laughed out loud. Hattie looked stern.

"When Eden crossed the Atlantic exhausted, Supermac came forward!" Mr Hague exhorted to wild Tory cheers. Even Alistair Darling now was fighting the giggles. Hattie was stony faced. "This could be your moment! While the Prime Minister is away, will you step in and make sure these schemes, on which so much economic confidence depends, are actually implemented now?"

Little Miss PC Plod chided Mr Hague to stop focusing on "political gossip". Mr Hague said that she shouldn't disparage her campaign. "That is not how to go about winning the leadership!"

Labour MPs hooted (they are only catatonic when Harriet is speaking) as Mr Hague's own stint as Tory leader did not end in success. He retorted: "I'm only a deputy now but at least I'm a loyal one!"

The plodding became so severe that I lost the will to record it. There was some excitement when Harriet said that the hated Sir Fred Goodwin had got his knighthood for his services to charity, not banking. Can that be true? It seemed unlikely.

Then Harriet had a — dare I say? — moment of genius when she turned to Mr Hague: "It wasn't only Sir Fred who was getting money off RBS, it was also you. You got £30,000 off the Royal Bank of Scotland for just two after-dinner speeches!"

Labour MPs, startled out of a deep sleep, screamed. Mr Hague blushed. From my perch above him, I could see his bald head glowing like a neon sign. It was a riotous 32 seconds of triumph, short but certainly sweet.

But then even that was ruined. Moments after Harriet left the chamber, she had to admit that Sir Fred's knighthood was for banking. Her 32 seconds were wiped off the clock. Little Miss Plod was back to zero. Gordon will be pleased.

10 March

Mandelson is unruffled by mere trifles

To watch Lord Mandelson toy with the MPs on the European Scrutiny Committee (many of whom are beyond eccentric) was a complete treat.

At first when I saw Lord Mandelson sauntering down the corridor, by himself, to the European Scrutiny Committee, I did not recognise him, for I have never seen him without an entourage. I had thought it would have to be surgically removed. Apparently not. But surely, after the incident last weekend when a protester threw green custard on him, he should have more, not less, security.

"I'm not sure what I'm doing here," he announced languidly to the corridor. Someone suggested it may be to do with Prime

Minister's favourite slogan: British jobs for British workers. He pursed his lips as if this thought had never occurred to him.

"Really?" he said in faux wonderment.

The Mandy magic continues. The room was full. This has never happened before to the European Scrutiny Committee. Usually if they have an audience of one, it is considered a crowd.

"I'm not sure what to call you," said Michael Connarty, the chairman.

"Call me anything," soothed Mandy.

"Mr Green!" cried an MP.

"Green Warrior!" chortled Mandy who, I now noticed, was dressed top to toe in a shade of veridian, looking not unlike a stylish if rather tall leprechaun. He had come prepared: any custard would simply blend in.

It is hard to describe the European Scrutiny Committee without using the words "mad as a box of frogs". (Although, even as I type the word "frogs", I am aware that some MPs will object on the grounds that I am being too French.) But then all its members have to have an obsession with the minutiae of Euro-drivel.

Mandy began by explaining that we live in a Euro-topia. Since 2001, he noted, 600,000 more British citizens have jobs. This shows that Britain has only benefited from workers from the new EU countries in 2004 and 2007.

"Over nine out of every ten people in employment are UK nationals. One can only conclude there has not been an adverse effect on the employment of British nationals," said Mandy, using leaps of logic that would impress a frog of any nationality.

The first to throw the green custard was James Clappison, a Tory. He objected to the use of the 600,000 figure from 2001.

This, he noted angrily, was three years before any new countries joined. A more relevant date was 2004, he said, and since then the number of employed British workers has dropped by 200,000.

"That is not a very substantial number," Mandy said airily.

Mr Clappison disagreed. He added that, since 2004, the number of migrants working had grown "very substantially". He said that Lord Mandelson had used a misleading statistic. Mandy said that it was not misleading. What happened next was nothing less than a food fight. As it wore on, I noticed that no food was sticking to Mandy. By the end, poor Mr Clappison was as green as an alien (the kind from Mars, not Europe).

The next one with a pie in his hand was Bill Cash, who is so obsessive that he speaks an entirely different language, not so much Esperanto as Euro-ranto. I am told by translators that he was asking yesterday if EU law should be changed to ensure that all workers in Britain should be paid according to agreed pay rates and not, merely, the minimum wage.

"There are no proposals," said Lord Mandy, utterly dismissive. "The Government has not discussed it."

Mr Cash spluttered as the green gloop hit him in the face. Mandy's face didn't move.

13 March

Harriet puts on her running stilettos

The leadership shenanigans surrounding Harriet Harman continued as she flirted outrageously with the Shadow Leader, also known as Hunky Dunky.

Harriet Harman is running for the Labour leadership. How do

I know? It all came out in a lovers' tiff in the Commons yesterday. For weeks Commons leader Harriet and her Tory shadow, Alan Duncan, have continued cooing at each other over the dispatch box. The fact that Hunky Dunky is gay and that Harriet is known as Harperson is beside the point. It is all too obvious that they adore each other.

It could almost be a Mills & Boon plot. Actually, it probably is. Dashing, suave, flirtatious Tory man decides to woo ambitious, po-faced, bluestocking Labour woman. He talks seductively at the dispatch box about Valentine's Day cards. She giggles. He heaps praise upon her talents. She laughs coquettishly. When critics assail her putative leadership bid, he offers a comforting hug and a heart-shaped chocolate. (I am not making this up.) She responds by saying it is he who should be promoted.

Yes, I know, yuck. We are in major sick-bag territory here and, for weeks, I have been hoping it would all just go away. Yesterday I realised it would not.

It began, as it so often does, with heaping mashed potato mounds of mutual adoration. Hunky teased Harriet about one of her old T-shirts that said: "This is What a Feminist Looks Like". Harriet glared at him provocatively as MPs tittered. (Fiona Mactaggart, a rather fearsome Labour backbencher, shouted at Hunky: "Oh for God's sake!")

Hunky brandished a copy of the *Mirror* that featured an interview with Hattie. "May I congratulate you for being in the centrefold? In the past you have said that you think Prime Ministers' wives ought to buy their clothes at Primark. Now you say that you love stilettos and shop there yourself."

At this Harriet leaned down to inspect her black patent leather stilettos. (Again, I am not making this up.)

"I'm more Savile Row, I have to admit," flounced Hunky.

"Might we conclude that this is preparation for you becoming prime minister yourself?"

Hattie looked stern. She took off her spectacles (I'm sure that, in Mills & Boon, she would "rip" them off). He had, she noted, as prim as a Victorian teapot, referred to the rumours of her leadership bid. "I say to you there is not one shred of truth, not one iota of truth in any of the suggestions ..."

Hunky looked stricken and moaned: "No-o-o-o!"

Harriet ploughed on: "... that have been made and that have been circulated in the newspapers."

My, but she was over-egging this. The phrase "circulated in the newspapers" sounded as if it was out of a movie. "While we can't stop the newspapers reporting them, at least you can respect what I say to you and not continue to make those accusations and, yes, I am wearing my stilettos today."

Hunky loved that. So did MPs. For the first time, I am convinced that Harriet really is running for the leadership. Indeed, I would go so far as to say that her denial proves it.

18 March

Hero lets his halo slip

Lord Myners, the City Minister, was the man who failed to find out about Fred the Shred's pension arrangements though, as he sees it, that certainly wasn't his fault

There is no doubt after yesterday that Lord Myners sees himself as one of the good guys in the Sir Fred Goodwin pension saga. When the time comes for the movie — and make no mistake, this is Spielberg territory — Paul Myners will expect to be one of the heroes. How do I know? Because he told us so.

Lord Myners, with his bristly white hair, fleshy face and City-slicker CV, seems an unlikely angel. But then God and Mammon work in mysterious ways and there is no doubt that the City Minister veers towards the metaphysical. "I think companies should have a soul," he told us at one point. "They should have a moral purpose."

Yes, OK, but what about Sir Fred? Lord Myners set the scene: it was the second weekend in October and the British banking system was collapsing. He was toiling away, halo glowing, in the bowels of the Treasury, working 24/7 from Friday until early Monday morning. Our hero and others were negotiating with eight major finance institutions, throwing billions around like confetti, saving the banking world. In the midst of all this grand drama was the tiny detail of Fred the Shred's pension at RBS. Lord Myners had had a "script" for this: he'd told RBS that there was to be no reward for failure and that was absolutely clear.

John McFall, the Treasury Select Committee chairman, said drily: "Outlining your principles is not the same as engaging in proper checks. Did you demand to see the relevant documents?"

Lord Myners hadn't for he was too busy saving the world but he had been told by RBS: "The pension will be enormous, you know that."

And he did know that. For, as he explained, that was the way of the City. He never thought that RBS might behave in anything less than a principled manner. There were "distinguished" people on its board.

Well, asked the Labour MP George Mudie, given what happened, didn't you slip up? "With all due respect ..." said Lord Myners.

Mr Mudie interrupted: "That means with no respect ..."

Lord Myners insisted that he had huge respect for Mr Mudie. "But I do not think that I slipped up. The right approach was one based around principles."

But, noted Mr Mudie, Sir Fred, with his £697,000-a-year pension, was rewarded for failure. "You were the minister who was handling that. You can't say it was nothing to do with you."

Lord Myners, who was beginning to sound prissy, protested: "I set very clear parameters and principles."

Mr Mudie asked again: "But surely, you must see that you slipped up?"

But Lord Myners did not. "Mandy Rice-Davies would probably anticipate my answer. I've looked very carefully at my own mind about this issue. I have asked myself, did I do something wrong, should I have done something differently? I have concluded that it was right to adopt an approach of setting up very clear principles."

Mr Mudie grumbled that Lord Myners had been "bloody naive".

Lord Myners retorted: "That question should be directed to the directors of the RBS."

There is no doubt whom Lord Myners thinks is the Devil in all this. At times he did all but put horns and a tail on Sir Fred and others at RBS. He even said it wasn't too late for Sir Fred to repent. I could hear the cackle all the way from Scotland on that.

But, even as he attacked, Lord Myners couldn't quite keep the sneaking admiration out of his voice. It was outrageous, it was wrong, it was breathtaking. But then suddenly Lord Myners, halo slipping, declared: "One has to admire, in a non-approving sense, the dexterity of Sir Fred Goodwin in respect of his own contract." Does one? I don't think so.

19 March

A rowdy, childish and cruel PMQs

The phoney war between Dave and Gordo erupted with much smoke, fire, bellowing and screams of joy. How MPs love it when they get to hate each other quite so much!

Prime Minister's Questions yesterday was back to "normal", by which I mean pugilistic, childish, wild, rowdy, cruel, funny and very, very loud. They call it a bear pit but that is an insult to bears and possibly pits. But MPs were absolutely loving it, for it has been a month since there was a Punch-and-Punch PMQs.

David Cameron was nervous, his hands shaking at times. He seemed a bit rusty but then perhaps he has forgotten what a formidable foe the PM can be. I suspect that Gordon, saviour of the world, doesn't care much about piddly little PMQs any more and that this has freed him. He is like a human pillbox: immovable, square, impervious.

There was no lack of ammo. Dave chucked the unemployment figures at Gordon who chucked them right back, saying that unemployment was higher in France, Germany, Japan and America.

Dave had another go, piling on the predictions of woe. "So, wasn't it wrong to claim that Britain was one of the best-placed countries in the world to withstand recession. Admit it?"

But Gordon would rather dance the tango in a G-string: "No, because the fact is that America entered recession more than a year and three months ago. The euro area entered recession in April last year. We entered recession in July."

Corrections flew around the chamber like swallows at dusk. It was all rather tedious. Indeed, Dave was quoting the German Chancellor (yes, that bad) when he had the sense to interrupt himself and look over at the always-sniping Dennis Skinner.

"You should be quiet," Dave shouted at Dennis. "I know you wanted miners to join the Government. Well, you've got him now — Lord Myners!" Up in the gallery, Lord Myners, the man who failed to spot Sir Fred Goodwin's mega-pension, looked down on a scene of chaos. This appalling joke had jolted MPs into non-stop hilarity.

Dave chortled: "The trouble is they all want Lord Myners to negotiate their retirement packages!" This led to even more screams of excitement.

Insults rained down on Gordo whose irritation boomed out: "You do not understand one thing. This is an unprecedented global banking crisis. Unprecedented means without precedent."

Labour MPs loved this. Gordon, emboldened, began to read out tedious quotes from this person and that. Dave counter-quoted (this is actually a verb now) by quoting something Gordon had said about, yes, quoting.

Dave threw down the paper. "What WHAT WHAT a complete phoney!"

Gordon pursed his lips into an unhappy pout. (Sometimes he really is rather camp.) The Speaker, waking up, said: "Let me chair the proceedings! That remark should be withdrawn and properly withdrawn!" Dave, chuckling, said he was happy to withdraw that. "Perhaps I can return to the Germans ..." Oh dear. Must we? Is it really that bad?

20 March
Edinburgh Jones and the Temple of Foam

Alistair Darling can make anything — even the Temple of Doom — seem dull. Here I tried to fight off sleep in order to figure out how he does it.

The most surreal moment of Alistair Darling's session in front of the Commons Treasury Select Committee came when the soft-spoken Labour MP Jim Cousins said: "Chancellor, if you are going to lead us into this Temple of Doom I think the British people will be looking to you to behave a little bit more like Indiana Jones."

Mr Darling's mouth opened and then closed. His eyebrows, which have been trimmed but still look like giant black caterpillars, just ones with recent haircuts, shot up. The room tittered.

I tried to imagine Mr Darling, hat askew, shirt open, racing across a rope bridge. Simply not possible. I could only see him as Edinburgh Jones, wearing a suit (trouser legs rolled up), creeping along, each eyebrow fastened to the bridge by bungee jump cables. Behind him crawled an army of aides, with binders.

It wasn't an action film so much as an inaction one. Perhaps that is why no one has ever made a movie called Edinburgh Jones and the Temple of Debt. Now, back in the jungle that is Westminster, Mr Edinburgh emitted a strange gurgling noise. "I could, get, um ..." Then, he said: "Suffice it to say I just don't agree with your analysis and your conclusion."

Mr Darling was up before the committee for two hours. It is amazing how he can say so much and so little at the same time.

His voice acts as a narcotic (it should be licensed and kept locked in a cupboard). By the end, almost everyone in the room looked stunned, as if they had been hit by a poison blowfish dart. I forced myself to stay alert to figure out how he does it.

My conclusion? At first I thought he was just good at being bland, a blancmange with eyebrows attached, but he is far more skilled than that. For Mr Darling is a smotherer. He takes every question and, acting in exactly the same way as fire-retardant foam, covers it with gloop until the question is extinguished.

Take executive pay. The Labour MP Nick Ainger noted that in America President Obama had imposed a $500,000 salary ceiling at banks that are receiving government cash. Why didn't Mr Darling do something similar here?

Mr Darling emitted a plume of words. There were "inheritance" problems with pay. But he wanted no reward for failure. That was exactly right. Actually did the committee know we had gone farther than America. What he wanted to do most was to protect the bank employees who earned very little. They were the troops! There was a huge gulf between them and those at the top.

Mr Ainger, fighting the foam, flickered into life: "Don't you think you should be setting an example?"

Mr Darling went into über-smother mode: "Firstly, if you look at the banking remuneration generally over the last 20 years ..."

And if we capped pay, then our bankers might be lured away by higher salaries elsewhere! "We have also got to make sure that we don't end up with a situation where other banks start attracting people who are key to making, say, RBS and the Lloyds Group work in the future," Mr Darling foamed. If they went elsewhere then, perhaps, we couldn't sell our banks back.

It sounded improbable but, by then, the foam had

overpowered us. It was a very careful performance. Mr Darling, halfway across the rope bridge, does not want any quick movements. Below him, the abyss awaits — although he does, of course, have his eyebrows firmly anchored.

— ENDS WINTER —

AN INFERNAL SPRING

Spring rushed in but found itself trying desperately to keep up with the pace of events. At Westminster, it felt like we were on a white water raft ride on a raging river, totally unmapped, with no one steering and with regular screams of "Man Overboard". If it wasn't the economy, it was MPs expenses which had been lurking for months (years actually) but now exploded into the news in April and May in relentless incredible voyeuristically fascinating detail. Gordon Brown may only remember his G20 triumph but the rest of us will remember YouTube, moats, manure and, of course, the gorgeous Joanna Lumley trouncing the government.

25 March

Gnomic Merv gives MPs the swerve

This was the momentous session when Mervyn King stabbed Gordon Brown in the front over his fiscal stimulus but, first, we had to wade through the counter-factual

Bank of England Governor Mervyn King, short and round, blinking behind his rimless specs, looks a bit like a gnome and, yesterday, before the Treasury Select Committee, he got more and more gnomic. By the end I was thinking that he must avoid pointy hats or he'll end up in a garden.

First, he was asked about the plight of savers. "That is what I call the Paradox of Policy," he announced, pudgy hands clasped.

Ah yes, the Paradox of Policy. I think that means something that makes no sense to real people. Alan Greenspan, his former fellow central banker, once said: "If I turn out to be particularly clear, you've probably misunderstood." Exactly.

It is with this in mind that I tell you Merv's catch-phrase, which is: "It is very hard to know the counter-factual." He dropped this in willy-nilly, using it like a comfort blanket.

Merv had only told us twice about the counter-factual when he was asked about QE — quantitative easing or, as I like to think of it, queasing — where the Bank prints money to buy assets. Why, asked Sir Peter Viggers, a Tory, was this better than, say, throwing money out of the helicopter? Mervyn explained that over the next three months he's going to spend £75 billion using a "twin-track" approach. It's all about increasing Broad Money (and no, that's nothing to do with women).

The first involves buying directly from companies. "That's what I call the Unconventional Unconventional purchases," said Merv.

I snorted, but immediately realised that I was alone in thinking that unconventional unconventionals were in any way unconventional. No one else in the room even moved a facial muscle.

Mr King blinked gnomically.

Was he channelling Donald Rumsfeld? Were unconventional unconventionals the new known knowns?

The second track of quantitative easing is to buy government bonds. "These are conventional unconventional purchases," explained Mr King-Greenspan-Rumsfeld to the row of nodding men.

So why £75 billion? Mr King conceded the correct amount is unknown (surely that should be known unknown.) "It's very hard to quantify," said Mr King. "It would be false precision to try." So, how will you know when it is working? "It is very hard to know what the counter-factual is," countered Mr King.

There was a discussion about the alphabet and which letter the recession would resemble. Options include V, L and U. Mr King is a V man. We're in V free-fall now.

"Since last summer," said Mr King, "the Panic of 2008 as I call it." (I immediately felt that the Panic of 2008 had to be connected to the Paradox of Policy: what a shame the recession cannot be P-shaped.) By next year, apparently, we'll be climbing up the other side of the V.

We were deep in the counterfactual when, suddenly, the Sage of Threadneedle Street stopped speaking in runes. The occasion was a question about whether the Government should consider a second fiscal stimulus (the first being the controversial VAT cut). "I'm sure the Government will want to be cautious," warned Mr King. We were facing very large deficits.

"The fiscal position of the UK is not one which says, 'Well why don't we just go on another significant round of fiscal expansion'."

As he said this, I could actually see, behind him, the spectre of Gordon Brown, who adores fiscal stimuli of all kinds, exploding. "We can do more monetary easing if necessary," said Mr King, placid as a pool, as he reverted to his gnomic ways. Ah yes, just what we need: more unconventional unconventionals to give us V for Victory.

27 March
Don't Bank on It, Episode 3

The government soap opera continues with Alistair Darling claiming to love Mervyn King though, of course, we all know that can't really be the case. Or can it?

It is getting hard not to see the Government's economic strategy as a soap opera. Title suggestions on a postcard, please (keep it clean), though I rather like something like Don't Bank on It. After Treasury Questions yesterday, I certainly wouldn't bank on anything, for the plot, as they say, has thickened.

Our story so far this week. It began with the Prime Minister fleeing to South America, where he and his Business Secretary, Lord Mandelson, were accused of making policy while wearing Speedo swim trunks. In their absence, Mervyn King, the Governor of the Bank of England, mounted a fiscal policy coup and then, to cap it off, dropped in on the Queen. Gordon, below the Equator, spluttered.

This brings us to Episode 3, Treasury Questions, yesterday in the House of Commons. It stars Alistair Darling, who often confuses viewers as he is at times played by a cardboard cutout. The studio audience is full of questions. Does Darling hate Merv? Does Darling hate Gordon? Does Gordon think Merv and Darling are out to get him? And what about the Queen? What do the corgis think of a global fiscal stimulus?

Cue gloomy cliffhanger music. Alistair is on the front bench, his white hair thinning and his beetling eyebrows reduced to baby beetle status. Behind him the Labour benches are as green as a fairway. It's got so bad that no one wants to be seen with him any more. Across sits his adversary, George Osborne, the Shadow Chancellor and all-round Tory scorpion.

MPs asked if Mr Darling agreed with Merv the Swerve that Britain was too much in debt for another fiscal stimulus. Mr Darling, picking his words as carefully as someone with a nut allergy approaches a box of Roses, said he and Merv agreed on many things. They both want jobs. They both "support" the economy (since when did the economy become a football team?). The Tories laughed.

But did Mr Darling agree our debt was too high to afford another financial stimulus?

"That actually wasn't what the Governor said," said Mr Darling (though it was).

George Osborne read out Merv's words of betrayal and, looking across the chamber, demanded: "In one word, would you tell us whether you agree with him — yes or no?"

Mr Darling came back with 168 words, none of them yes or no. He launched into an encomium about Merv and him. They were in "complete agreement" about what happened last November. They were in "complete agreement" about the G20.

And, oh yes, they were in "total agreement" also. They were like those married couples who never fight. "It's you that is the problem, not us!" Mr Darling cried.

Mr Osborne sneered, at which he excels. He read out the Merv quote again — this was like torture by quotation — and asked, again, if Mr Darling agreed.

This pushed Mr Darling into yet another clothes drenching gush (the overacting in this soap opera is atrocious!). The problem wasn't Merv. The problem wasn't debt or credit. Oh no! The problem was George and his "youthful impetuousness". He said it as if it were a crime, which, for all I know, it may be in Merv's Brave New World.

So, at the end of this episode, it's chaos.

31 March

Dumbfermline has dunloanin'

Another day, another bail-out. As the Dunfermline Building Society is rescued, MPs blamed the Chancellor who blamed the management who, of course, blamed the Chancellor

Alistair Darling began his statement on the Dunfermline Building Society, which is now very much a dunloanin' one, by declaring that he held accounts for his children at the society. This made me remember that when we bailed out Northern Rock, Mr Darling revealed that he had a mortgage there. I wonder if he had an Icelandic account too? Or, perhaps, an RBS credit card? Whatever the opposite of the Midas touch is, he's got it.

It is Mr Darling's job to make the fact that he has just written a £1.6 billion cheque to the Nationwide to take over the Dunloanin' seem perfectly normal. Thus he began by announcing: "It will be business as usual for customers." I am not sure the phrase "business as usual" is consoling these days.

We then had what is becoming our daily fix of financial porn: the grisly details of how it had all gone so incredibly wrong. Basically, and I paraphrase the Chancellor but not much, the Dunfermline had been the Dumbfermline (sorry but it's true).

They had gone into commercial property lending, to the tune of £650 million, at exactly the wrong time. Then they had bought, and this takes a certain kind of reverse genius, £150 million of repackaged British, high-risk, self-certified mortgages from two American firms, one of which was a subsidiary of Lehman Brothers. They did this just before the global market for these loans and, not incidentally, Lehman, collapsed.

Mr Darling did not say but I think we now own all those debts or, as they say, "hold" them. He explained this by saying that the Treasury was following normal practice. It is a sign of the times that there is a "normal practice" for toxic debt so that failed building societies can conduct "business as usual". "What is the maximum possible loss to the taxpayer?" asked George Osborne, the Shadow Chancellor. "You mentioned a small residual exposure. How small is it?" Too small to mention, apparently, for Mr Darling didn't.

There were only seven Labour backbenchers there. The Tories were mob-handed. Gordon Brown, global warrior and former MP for Dunfermline, was entertaining El Presidente de México and too busy to attend.

"Isn't the extraordinary thing that the provision of another £1.6 billion worth of public money to rescue another failed institution no longer seems extraordinary," Michael Fallon, the self-appointed Tory grandee, said. How, he demanded, did the regulator let this happen?

Mr Darling did not know. Rather unnervingly, Mr Darling

can hardly seem to believe it himself. "It comes back to this point that comes up time and time again — whether it's Bradford & Bingley, RBS, HBOS. The question has to be asked, what was the management doing? What questions were being asked. When people said, 'Well the money seems to be coming in here,' surely someone was asking: 'How?'"

Well, Chancellor, apparently no one did ask that question. MPs desperately tried to blame someone, anyone would do. Some blamed the Chancellor who blamed the management who blamed the Chancellor and, of course, Lord Myners (another one with a reverse Midas touch, I think).

Bernard Jenkin, matinee idol and Tory MP, was "absolutely clear" that capitalism was not to blame.

Mr Darling said drily: "This is probably not an occasion to dwell on the future of capitalism."

Probably not. So would there be any more such occasions? Are there any other building societies similarly exposed? And where do the Darlings hold an account? The Chancellor refused to say. It seems that he is not dunbailin' yet.

1 April
If only it was an April's Fool

The Prime Minister gave a sermon in St Paul's Cathedral and, lo, but he was loud.

The Twyford gospel choir swayed from side to side. "Take control!" they sang, in perfect harmony. Oh no, I thought, don't encourage him. For somewhere, lurking in the transepts of St Paul's Cathedral, Gordon Brown was waiting to preach (sorry, speak) to us on the eve of the blessed G20.

"Hallelujah!" cried the choir. Truly, this must be Gordon's idea of heaven. No one in Labour treats him like this any more. The press were on high, at angel height. We had a perfect view of the Prime Minister, son of a manse, as he began his sermon.

And lo, but he was loud. The Prime Minister, standing beneath what may be the most glorious dome in the world, boomed forth. As one bellowed word overlapped the next, I felt that even God would have to turn down His hearing aid.

For Gordon, this was a deeply revealing speech. A Presbyterian by nature and nurture, he remains chary of religious fervour but, for him, the global economic crisis is a morality tale that needs telling and retelling. His role seems to be that of a Moral Maze Moses for he is busily creating a new set of commandments, which he calls "shared global rules".

"Markets need morals," he intoned. These, then, will be among the G20 Commandments: thou shalt not use tax havens, thou shalt not reward failure, thou shalt reshape the global financial system. (The tablet-chisellers will be busy, for Mr Brown will never stop at ten.) At the core of the "new global ethic" are the values of the family and the politics of the "kitchen table summit". It is very old-fashioned, more Waltons than Simpsons.

Moral, moral, moral. It was the most used word in the speech. He talked of religions — Christians, Jews, Muslims, Buddhists, Sikhs and Hindus all got name checks — but in a moral sense. "We all feel the same deep sense that each of us is our brother and sister's keeper." Now Mr Brown could not resist name-checking his own heroes.

"Call it, as Adam Smith did, the moral sentiment, as Lincoln did the better angels of our nature, as Winstanley did the light in man. Call it duty or simply conscience — it means we cannot and will not pass by on the other side when people are suffering." The speech was almost a half hour. I fear the angels nodded off at one point but Gordon, looking out on an audience of 2,000 including two Grand Muftis, did a Bill Clinton. It was Mr Clinton who gave us "ubuntu", an African word that means "I am because you are".

Now Mr Brown explained how economists once told the poor they must follow the free market because of Tina (There Is No Alternative). But campaigners fought Tina with Themba: There Must Be An Alternative.

"In that cry — Themba! — we hear everything that must guide us today," he said, adding that the acronym was also a Zulu word for the most important thing humans could have. "Hope!" he cried in a rather un-Presbyterian way.

"Themba — the confidence, conviction, and certainty that where there are problems there are always solutions." So there you have it, a new quasi-religion, called Themba, in which people around a kitchen table tell bankers not to be so greedy. Add a few limos, photo calls and up to £50 million for lots of bumf on how not to be greedy, and it sounds like the G20 to me.

2 April
Obama-tastic day for Gordon

President Obama was in town for the G20 and, unlike his first meeting with Mr Brown in Washington, this one was full of razzmatazz, flags, pomp and ceremony. Gordon was very close to heaven.

President Obama, who had seemed rather cool towards Gordon Brown in Washington a few weeks ago, went the other way yesterday. He showered Mr Brown with praise: the special relationship was extraordinary, lasting, wonderful.

And Britain itself was wonderful — and sunny! And, oh yes, he loves the Queen! They are over the surname stage now. It's all Barack this and Gordon that. Gordon told us that Barack was his personal friend. Then Barack told us that Gordon was his new best friend. Gordon looked at him adoringly. We are talking labrador here.

The event had begun nervously. Gordon's opening speech was as rushed as a groom late for the church. In contrast the President was positively languid. He offered little titbits of personal info. He'd had a chat with Gordon's sons about dinosaurs. At one point he began swigging from a water bottle.

Gordon began to relax. His face, which seemed overly made up with rather pouting orangey lips, looked almost bashful. It occurred to me that this event may be the apex of his political career. He looked transported. On his recent visit to Washington the White House had not even allowed him a press conference: instead there had been a "pooled spray" where hacks shouted at the leaders from behind a sofa. But yesterday Gordon got his press conference big-time.

It was in the Locarno room, a bling-fest of Empire. There were lecterns, flags (eight), hundreds of journalists, lights, cameras, action. In the front row, Hillary Clinton, in blinding blue, was accompanied by Davey Miliband (minus trademark banana).

Now we know what comes after the pooled spray: the total gush. Old Faithful, the geyser at Yellowstone, would be jealous of the sheer force of the output. This, for instance, was Gordon. "It's been an extraordinary visit already and I've benefited from Barack's advice not just about elections, but about fitness! We've been talking, not the treadmill of politics but the treadmill that we're both on every day, the running machines!"

Barack gushed back. The sheer level of his charm is

fascinating. This, for instance, was his take on President Sarkozy's petulant threat to walk out of the G20. It was all a media fantasy. "I know that when you've got a bunch of heads of state talking, it's not visually that interesting," said Mr Obama. "So there's a great desire to inject some conflict and some drama into the occasion. But the truth of the matter is I think there has been an extraordinary convergence!"

The media fantasy didn't seem quite so imaginary a few hours later at the day's other main event — the Sarko-Merkel press conference. If the morning event was dignified and adult, this was playtime. The children were not very happy. They have "red lines" and they want them met. They want tax havens named and shamed, hedge funds regulated, financial transparency. "This is nothing to do with ego or temper tantrums," said Sarko as he stamped his tiny (well, OK, *petit*) foot. I could almost hear Gordon and his new best friend laughing about that.

3 April

(Almost) making history in a giant tin can

The G20 was an utterly ghastly event to cover, sequestered, as we were in one bit of the giant tin can that is the ExCeL centre. Still, Gordon was ecstatic …

To the ExCeL centre, then, to see history being made. Actually it wasn't quite that easy. The day began like a novel as we were bundled off a "dirty" bus in a godforsaken car park in Peruvian Wharf, East London, so named because this was where they used to unload the guano. It seemed appropriate, somehow.

We clambered on to a "clean" bus (spy-talk for security-cleared) and were driven through a landscape like Mars with litter. We got off this bus and were directed on to another. Eventually, we staggered into the grievously misnamed ExCeL, slightly triumphant to have made it this far.

When I was growing up I used to read a history series called I Was There. Well, finally I was there but it seemed that history was actually 200 yards down the hall in the Red Zone. I, as a Yellow Zoner, was banned. Still, if journalism is the first draft of history, then this, written in a stiff breeze in this hangar-like place, is at least the first draught.

The best way to explain the ExCeL centre is to imagine a giant tin can on its side. We could not see out, which, given the view, may not have been such a bad thing. In the Yellow Zone we were visited by Red Zoners whom we treated like demi-gods, for we were desperate for news. When Alistair Darling came over he was mobbed. Yes, I know, that is unbelievable, but that is a bit of history that I saw.

As the day wore on, everyone began to talk about an extra trillion dollars for the world. No one seems to know how this is possible when we're all so broke, but such questions were viewed as idiotic.

The Canadians missed the first "family photo" (I can't believe anyone noticed) and Berlusconi the second. Did this happen at Bretton Woods? How can they save the world if they can't even take a group photo? Peter Mandelson, slumming it in the Yellow Zone canteen, when asked what it was like to be at the fulcrum of history, said: "The soup's nice." It was, for the record, watercress.

The person everyone was talking about, though, was Sarko. He was late for dinner the night before because he had to "freshen up". Now the rumour was that his make-up artist was marooned outside. *Quelle horreur*! He was having to make history without his slap! No wonder he was in a mood.

At 3 pm we heard that the communiqué, which everyone called "the text", was nearing completion. Gordon's moment of glory — the apex, the acme, the summit of his political life — was set for 3.30 pm. Then, suddenly, Sarko moved his press conference forward, to clash with Gordon's.

Why? "He's in a hurry," a spokesman said. Well, he was in a something. It all felt slightly out of control. In the end Gordon strode on to the stage at 3.56 pm with the words: "This is the day the world came together." Well, not quite, For next door, Sarko had started his version of his G20 *triomphe* (it was his idea, as you may know). Gordon was measured, dignified, a bit dull.

Sarko was ebullient, sharp and highly entertaining. I ran between the two. History had been made, but who knows whose story it will be? I was there and I can confirm this at least: the soup was nice.

21 April

It's Jacqui Smith, not quite unplugged

The Easter break was fraught for the Home Secretary: the leaked details of her expenses revealed she had charged the taxpayer for, among other things, a barbecue, a toothbrush holder, scatter cushions, a bathplug, and two porn films. Upon returning to Westminster, she had to face the Commons over the arrests of terror suspects.

Jacqui Smith seems to have taken her inspiration for her Commons performance from something very dear to her heart — her bathplug. She has not spent our 88p in vain.

Yesterday the Home Secretary took that object — the

cleanest item by far on her now infamous expenses — and used it to plug her mouth.

It was a move of genius. Indeed, I would be surprised if the word "bathplugging" does not become a political verb that is acknowledged as the best possible way to fight leaks of all kinds.

Ms Smith chose her topic well yesterday. By this, I mean that she picked one that she could not talk about by law. Yes, by law, as in contempt-of-court law. Thus she began her "statement" on the terror arrests with the words: "I'm sure the House will understand why I cannot go into detail."

But I'm not sure it mattered what the House thought, certainly not the Tories who were out in force to watch her squirm. For she kept to her word. No detail got past that bathplug. It was like listening to porridge. She was asked many questions — about Pakistan, about student visas, about border security — and gave us answers of total gloop. They all disappeared without a trace.

Chris Grayling, the Shadow Home Secretary, is a man made for the word lugubrious but he was no match for this. He noted that our Pakistan student visa assessment operation had been moved to Abu Dhabi. Why had she done this strange thing? She looked at him blankly: the bathplug was in. We never heard of Abu Dhabi again.

He tried to sneer, something at which he is very bad. "And if we believe the Downing Street rumour mill — despite everything, it does appear to be still operating — you will be on your way before long as well," he said in a voice close to monotone.

Ms Smith's face did not move. Downing Street rumours are the least of her worries. If it is true that what doesn't kill you makes you stronger, then Ms Smith is made of tungsten by now. It takes guts to live your life knowing everyone you meet can think of only one word and that is "porn". We used to look at Ms Smith and think cleavage, now it's porn. I suppose that is progress of sorts.

Her reaction to all of this seems to have become prim. There has always been something of the barmaid about Ms Smith but now, post-porngate, she was as prim as a headmistress facing a class of naughty boys. After Mr Grayling sat down, she scolded him: "The fact that you chose to spend a significant proportion of your response to my statement talking about me rather than the issue says rather more about you than it says about me." To this a Tory bellowed: "You ARE the issue!"

Her lips pursed. This was her answer to all. She came under attack from her own side about G20 and the arrest of the MP Damian Green, who sat, glowering at her throughout. In response, she pursed her lips, parting them only to emit more porridge.

This drove the Tory Douglas Hogg to distraction. "Do you understand my puzzlement about the fact that you have chosen to make a statement that is wholly empty?" he demanded. Her lips, pursed for so long that I feared some sort of cosmetic surgery had been involved, parted in a shadow of a smile. She and her bathplug had won the day.

22 April
Gordon, king of YouTube

The news that Gordo had announced his new policy on MPs expenses on YouTube seemed too incredible to be true. And then I watched it. Now that was incredible.

Gordon Brown made his announcement on MPs' expenses to

himself via a video camera from an empty room at No 10. I say himself but there must have been a camera there. And, in the background, there was a lovely white marble fireplace. I can see why he chose a fireplace as an audience: its reaction to everything is to say: "That's really, really grate!"

No 10 will be posting this fireplace chat on YouTube. It is probably hoping for five stars and lots of "Gr8!" comments. This seems unlikely as fireplaces can't type and the YouTube electorate can be brutal. (The last comment on Gordon's "I Saved the World" video yesterday was: "This scum should hang for treason.") Certainly it will be hard for this one to beat the popularity of his most-watched video, Gordon Brown Picking His Nose, which has 376,133 hits and 4.5 stars.

But this one is good in a bad sort of way. I think it is either five stars or one. There is no in between here. And I cannot discount the thought that this may be Mr Brown's foray into cinéma vérité as the camera wobbles quite a bit.

Actually that may be the PM wobbling: it's hard to tell with cinéma vérité. The video begins jerkily. You get the feeling that the PM was chatting happily to himself into a two-way mirror when, suddenly, someone (his therapist?) hit the wrong button.

He looks incredibly jolly. He is smiling and rocking a bit from side to side, as if he were on a donkey at the seaside (he may have been as we see him only from waist up). "Going round the country I have been struck by the comments that are made about young people when I meet them about what jobs they want to do when they grow up," he said, rocking, smiling, hands flapping away a bit like seal flippers.

I believe him. I have been round the country with the PM and he asks virtually everyone he meets what they want to be when they grow up. (It can be disconcerting for adults.) Yesterday Gordon, still smiling and swaying, told us that everyone wanted to be teachers and doctors and no one wanted to be an MP. "That is a shame," he said, inappropriate smile lurking like a shark in shallow waters.

The problem isn't MPs (the "vast majority" are fine) but the expenses system. "MPs need to have the humility to recognise that the country has lost confidence," he said. I think that the "vast majority" of MPs will find the idea of Mr Brown lecturing them on humility somewhat galling.

The PM had "urgent" proposals to fix the problem. He said that Harriet Harman — the therapist will have noted that at her name his entire body jerked into "dad-dancing" mode — had the details. He was there for the headlines (sorry, highlights).

The cinéma vérité got more vérité as he got mixed up with the autocue but, basically, he is scrapping the second-home allowance. Instead, MPs will receive extra money for coming to Parliament. He called this an "attendance" allowance. I think that is code for "showing up for work". Wow. Extra money for actually coming to work. This was a draconian crackdown.

There was lots more swaying and eyebrow action. Mr Brown's private party peaked when, as he told us that he wants MPs to approve his proposals next week, he almost burst into laughter.

So what's the rating? I'm with the fireplace here: it has to be five stars.

23 April

The Budget: Where is Munch when we need him?

Was it The Budget or was it the political equivalent of The Scream? Actually, it was both.

It's a good thing that Alistair Darling is so dull or else we'd all have run from the chamber screaming. The news wasn't bad, it was appalling. If Edvard Munch were painting today, he'd have to revise his most famous work The Scream to give his figure beetling bootblack eyebrows and a stream of astronomically long figures of debt coming out of his open mouth.

Actually, if Munch had been alive and listening to the Budget, he might have ended up slumped forward, face down in his fiercely pessimistic palette.

Mr Darling has that effect: there are South American frogs out there that are jealous of his ability to stun. When I was in the chamber listening, I knew things were awful but such was the soporific power of Mr Darling that I almost didn't care — which is, of course, just as well.

I've now had enough time to recover to give you the highlights. Er, actually, that's it. There were no highlights, only lowlights. How low can we go? Well, the best news of the day was that our exports may be down 14 per cent but that Germany's have plummeted 21 per cent and Japan's 45 per cent. Gordon Brown, sitting there with his arms, legs and probably fingers crossed, nodded. He loves these comparative lists in which we always win.

Mr Darling's family — wife, mother, son — were there to watch. They stayed awake but, don't forget, they have had practice (or, possibly, access to an antidote). After the cheering news on exports, Mr Darling gave us the desperate sounding debt figures to a Tory soundtrack of "Oh! Oh! Oh!" I think it was when he told us that it wasn't going to stabilise until 2015-16 that I wished that I had my very own tranquilliser gun.

History will record that the death of new Labour came at 1 pm on April 22, 2009, when Mr Darling said the words "the new tax rate will be 50 per cent".

Tony Blair — can it really be that he was still Prime Minister only two years ago? — will have a wry chuckle over that. Then he will have to take a call from a furious Cherie. The nouveaux riches Blairs will be among the losers of this Budget. That will make Gordon flash one of his funny peculiar grins (which surely Munch would capture in an equally spooky rendering called The Smile).

The whole event had the feeling of a session at the dentist, something that had to be got through, with Mr Darling acting as the novocaine. He sat down to half-hearted cheers from Labour backbenchers. Even the front bench looked like a clan meeting of The Grims. Mr Brown must have wished fervently to be transported back to his G20 day of triumph: no wonder he prefers the global stage these days.

The really bad news for Mr Brown, though, came next because David Cameron was on stonkingly good form. At first he seemed a bit shouty but then he hit his stride, ripping into Mr Brown's judgment, his errant predictions and "callous" boasts.

"What planet are these people on?" he cried. "They sit there, running out of money, running out of moral authority, running out of time. You have to ask what on earth is the point of another 14 months of this Government of the living dead?" It seems that after The Scream comes The Savaging. On this form, Mr Cameron is dangerous.

24 April

To boldly go ... somewhere

Ed Miliband, the younger brother of Dave, the Banana Man, may be the one who replaces Gordon in the end. For now, though, he's the greenest of them all.

To the Commons, then, for a bit of fantasy politics. Ed Miliband, the Climate Change Secretary, came to tell us how he is going to create green, coal-fired power stations. It is all very exciting.

There are going to be four of them and they are going to capture carbon and keep it under the North Sea, forever, where it can't harm anyone but the mermaids.

It was like science fiction but for real. Who needs to see the new Star Trek when you can watch this? I half expected to see Captain Kirk, or at least Scotty, in the Chamber.

Sadly not even Spock, who is a Tory, was there. I had to make do with the usual Klingons and John Gummer.

It seems appropriate that Ed Miliband is our secretary of state for science fiction. Both he and his brother, David, are talked of as future Labour leaders but I suspect Ed really IS the future. Indeed, if I had to bet which will come first — Ed as leader or coal as green as our valleys — I'd go for Ed.

The first thing to know about the future is that we have to talk in code. Everyone was warbling on about carbon capture and storage, also called CCS and carbon abatement (look, it's not my fault).

One Labour MP told Ed he must be on top of the "transformation agenda" for the "new black gold". Ed nodded and said he couldn't agree more.

Soon I came to realise that the "transformation agenda" is code for "have no idea if it's going to work but let's do it anyway". What Ed did yesterday was lay down strict rules in which the fantasy is to take place. So there will be new coal-fired stations but only on the condition that they pretend that they will be able to capture all their carbon by 2025. They are going to do this through something called retro-fitting (which has nothing to do with vintage clothing or Lieutenant Uhura).

Every coal-fired power station built from now would have to commit to retro-fitting the whole plant, 100 per cent, within five years of 2020, subject to the technology being ready, said Ed, whose words come out in a globular fashion, as round as all those molecules that he plans to imprison. The Lib Dems said that "subject to the technology being ready" was a "dirty great loophole". Ed frowned. Such pessimism has no place in Star Trek Green Enterprise where there is no dirt, as everything, even politics, is clean.

Greg Clark, the Shadow Climate Change Secretary, is the Tory for Tunbridge Wells. As such, he has to be disgusted and yesterday he duly was. He said that, until now, our energy policy has been a "horror show". (The Klingons grunted.) Greg said that Ed had copied his ideas and, just to prove how clever he is, he asked: "If four pilots are consented, each generating 300 megawatts of abated electricity, that will mean there will be 1.2 gigawatts of new capacity to be abated by 2020, how much unabated elecricity do you expect will be generated by 2020?" Everyone pretended they knew the answer. Why not? It's their fantasy. Ed ended by saying that he wanted "to boldly go" where no minister had gone before. Or did I just imagine that?

28 April

Tories re-arrange the deckchairs

Every once in a while, no matter how much you plan, an event goes totally wrong. Such was the Tory launch of their Euro-election campaign.

David Cameron and his team of Tory boys launched their Euro

election campaign at a place called The Deck at the National Theatre. It sounds a nautical, jaunty sort of "space" but the word that kept occurring to me as I walked there along the Thames in the cold driving rain was "Titanic".

This was confirmed when, upon arrival, I saw them rearranging the deck chairs. At least it was only a small disaster movie with only 30 chairs to accommodate the usual Tory rent-a-crowd: that is to say, attractive young women in sparkly earrings and important men in suits. In politics it is normal for men to outnumber women two to one, if not three to one: it was even more male yesterday though, perhaps in honour of Euro-day, the suits did seem better cut.

The Deck, which has glass walls and a floor of ribbed decking, was cold and wet and as close to being in the river as possible. Indeed, only the lack of breathing apparatus convinced me that we were above ground. That and the "urban seagulls" that wheeled around, circling over us like politicians in search of a policy.

As if on cue, Dave arrived. He swept in, utterly untouched by the weather. How does he do it? The man is getting smoother and smoother, as if he has been polished with sandpaper. I hate to think of the amount of derma-abrasion involved.

He was accompanied by William Hague, the Shadow Foreign Secretary, whose head shines like a billiard ball, and Eric Pickles, who is also round but very jiggly and makes an unmade bed look immaculate. Mr Pickles is the Tory party chairman, although his appearance and soft Yorkshire accent make him seem Labour to his core. He replaced Caroline Spelman. I don't miss her endless beigeness but now cannot help but notice that there is no longer even a token woman at these events. Where is Kate Winslet when we need her?

The disaster movie began in earnest now. Mr Pickles rolled up to speak but, as he opened his mouth, a helicopter flew directly over us. As the Drone invaded The Deck, I watched Mr Pickles's mouth open and close, like a pufferfish's. From the snatches I could hear, I think he was talking about keeping your promises. Needless to say, it wasn't long before he sat down.

Dave bounded up. He was standing in front of a terrifying poster that showed Gordon Brown with two faces joined by one ear. The ear looked very weird, like a mutant ear from horror sci-fi. The poster slogan was "Make Labour's next U-turn an EU-turn" but I was far too obsessed by the mutant ear to take that in.

Even Dave must have known he was starring in a Euro-disaster movie by now. He stood next to The Ear — I have never seen a mere lobe look so menacing — and did battle with The Drone as it came and went. As he spoke, he must have noticed that his wet audience, now getting warmer, was starting to steam gently.

He had a simple, not to say shallow, message, which was that the Tories want a referendum now. Dave, when asked lots of detailed questions, just kept chanting the word "now". "The best time for now is now," he said. Well, now, it's a washout.

29 April

Alfie and the politics of envy

It had been just under a week since the Budget and the new 50p tax rate had set off a rather thuggish class warfare among MPs. It was getting very personal indeed.

What's it all about, Alfie? Well, basically, what it was all about yesterday was Labour disgust at Sir Michael Caine's objection to the new 50p tax rate. At Treasury Questions, the rumbustious "Soak the Rich" Labour rump was jubilant.

"I read with some interest some certain celebrity millionaires like Sir Michael Caine are considering leaving the country because of the Government's tax," said Stephen Hepburn, who is so old Labour that he could be an item on the Antiques Roadshow.

The Tories were shouting, for we are in a nascent class war and it takes almost nothing to set them off. The Conservative benches looked like a stag do (29 men, two women). The front bench was pure testosterone with five men all in a row.

Their braying only fuelled Mr Hepburn who warned that Sir Michael and his rich celeb mates needed to remember something: "It's ordinary hard-working people who actually pay the money to watch their films who put them where they are. Can we give a message that if they cannot turn round and support services for those hard-working people such as the NHS when the country is going through a bit of a problem then good riddance to them!"

MPs catcalled as Mr Hepburn steeled himself and — in what can only be called an Oscar bid — shouted: "And don't come back!"

Alistair Darling, on the front bench for the first time since his Budget nightmare, looked alarmed. He knows that our finances are in such a parlous state that, without Sir Michael and his tax bill, the Chancellor would have to redo the Budget yet yet again (he's already redone it so many times that he is running out of red ink).

Stephen Timms, the Financial Secretary, a tall ungainly brainbox who speaks without any discernible passion, announced that he agreed with Mr Hepburn, but then added lamely: "I hope Michael Caine isn't going to leave the country."

I have to say that if Sir Michael was watching Parliament TV

— and where else can you pick up such top tips on over-acting? — then that would have had him heading for Heathrow.

I looked at the Labour benches for any members of the ever-shrinking New Labour tendency. Only the day before Stephen Byers, the arch-Blairite, had condemned the 50p rate. But yesterday he was nowhere to be seen.

Instead up popped Peter Kilfoyle, the almost entirely square MP for Liverpool Walton. He arose with a sneer: "Isn't it entirely consistent with Labour values and principles that those who benefited most over the last 15 years, like the 17 millionaires on the Tory front bench, that they should be the people to pay their fair share now that there is a downturn?"

Seventeen, huh? As Sir Michael might say: "Not many people know that." I certainly didn't. I looked anew at the five men on the Tory front bench and wondered who was the richest. George Osborne, Shadow Chancellor and millionaire, laughed. Next to him, Philip Hammond — tall, patrician and perhaps even more of a millionaire than Georgie — jumped up to tell us about his fears for the non-rich.

He claimed that there was a £45 billion black hole that meant £1,450 extra tax per year per family. This was a "secret Labour stealth tax bombshell".

I heard his words but found myself wondering instead about his bank balance. Who were the other millionaires? Brace yourself for a dose of the politics of envy. That, Alfie, is what this is really all about.

30 April

The Gurkhas surprise everyone

The government did everything it could — wheedle, bribe, cajole — to win the vote that would severely curtail the number of Gurkhas who could live here. And everyone thought they had won. Then, amazingly...

For a split-second, opposition MPs couldn't believe their eyes. They stared, goggle-eyed, as the tellers for the Gurkha vote lined up before the glittering mace in the Commons at 4.15 pm.

It had been a hell of a debate, the highlight being a blatant Labour bid to buy votes, all watched over by a luminescent Joanna Lumley. But now everyone could see, from the order the tellers stood in, that Labour's jiggery pokery hadn't worked. The Liberal Democrats, so used to losing, had won big.

Incredulity turned to a ragged, belting cheer — order papers fluttering like confetti. As the vote of 267 to 246 was read out, Nick Clegg's back was slapped so much that he began to list.

The government front bench looked almost ill. Phil Woolas, the Immigration Minister, had the stunned look of a rabbit with myxomatosis. He was speechless, possibly for the first time in his entire life.

I looked up to the gallery where Ms Lumley, whose father's life was saved by a Gurkha, had watched the entire messy debate, sitting next to a Gurkha with a medal on his lapel.

Minutes later, outside, Ms Lumley was transported with joy and looked, well, absolutely fabulous. "No more delays!" she cried as Nick Clegg and David Cameron grinned away like fools in love.

"I would like to thank the loving and lovely people of Great Britain," said one Gurkha — though, actually, he should have thanked the incompetent Government of Great Britain.

For yesterday I watched as they tried to buy this vote with promises galore. It was cack-handed, rudimentary Bribery 101 and, actually, I thought they'd done enough to win.

The debate began with fine words.

The Liberal Democrat home affairs spokesman, Chris Huhne, in his best speech ever, said that there was a reason the Gurkhas were called "bravest of the brave".

"This debate is not just about the Gurkhas. It is about the sort of people we are. Are we really to repay unconditional commitment with the penny-pinching approach of the accountant? Are we really the sort of people who know the price of everything and the value of nothing?"

The answer, provided momentarily by Mr Woolas, was "yes". He ducked and dived as he explained why there must be a limit on how many Gurkhas could stay here. Could we really afford to have them all? The Lib Dems lived in a fantasy world! "The Government has to live in the real world! Not the world of emotion," he noted. I wondered what had happened to the moral compass.

Labour whips were circling. Up popped George Howarth, Labour rebel. "There has been a lot of progress today," he said, listing various concessions including the inevitable review. "If you would go a little bit farther ..."

Guess what? Mr Woolas could! In a twinkling, a Labour MP handed round a piece of paper that I could see, from the logo, was from the Home Office. Mr Howarth read out the letter from the Home Secretary with — yes! — the coveted concession (the review would be over by August). Mr Howarth declared himself a happy man.

Others were not taken in. Keith Vaz warned Labour members that they were being naive. Michael Howard surprised all by giving an eloquent and moving speech.

In the background little groups of Labour MPs milled round, clutching the sacred letter. The whips were much in evidence for the vote. One of them, Ian Austin, stood by the "aye" lobby door and, whenever a Labour MP approached, pointed them the other way, towards the "no" door.

The rebels all just walked on by.

Still, I don't think they ever thought they'd win.

1 May

They're so vain — they probably think this sketch is about them

In the wake of the Prime Minister's exotically mad YouTube announcement, MPs gathered to debate yet again how to clean up their expenses. They seemed to be almost in pain and this, don't forget, was before the Telegraph began to reveal all.

"Every single member of this House is considered to be a crook!" cried David Heath, a Lib Dem. "It is something we have to deal with as a matter of urgency!"

MPs looked alarmed. This may be because Mr Heath, as the hairiest man in the chamber, now resembled an enraged Yeti. But it may also have been because he said the dread word "urgency". MPs love arguing about expenses but hate doing anything.

Now Barry Sheerman, a senior Labour backbencher, scolded the Yeti: "You are making me very angry because you haven't said one good thing about parliamentarians, the hard work we put in!" Mr Sheerman's entire body was shaking with indignation: "Come on! Please! Say something good about our colleagues!"

At this, the Yet had another temper tantrum.

Shambles is too kind a word for what happened yesterday. My, but it was grumpy — which is surprising, considering they were talking about their favourite subject; ie, themselves. We heard what time they got to work (7.30 am), what they did on Sunday mornings (church, golf or even dentistry) and how they are sometimes given bottles of wine for speaking engagements.

It occurred to me, as the personal details (in some cases practically CVs) rolled in, that MPs are so vain, they probably think this debate is about them. There were only a few who seemed to realise it was about us, the taxpayers. The Labour veteran Tony Wright, in a deeply thoughtful speech, observed that the public are so hostile that they wouldn't mind if MPs slept on benches in St James's Park. "But then they'd still say we were sleeping on someone else's bench!" he noted wryly.

The overriding mood was near despair. I don't know why, because Harriet Harman had already retreated on the core issue. This was the plan to scrap the second-home allowance and instead pay MPs for showing up, announced by the Prime Minister in his magnificently weird YouTube announcement (described yesterday as having the "awfulness of a David Brent announcement").

Harriet had even accepted an amendment, put forward by the Tory grandee Sir George Young, that, basically, sent all issues to do with MPs' expenses into the long grass that is Sir Christopher Kelly's review.

Thus the core decision, the decision not to decide, had been endorsed by all MPs.

With unanimity in danger of breaking out, MPs now set about picking a fight with each other with the intensity of a cat stalking a mouse. Within minutes, they pounced, saying that Harriet must cancel all other related votes (on subjects such as financial transparency). They argued, as fiercely as enraged teenagers, that the decision not to decide meant that it was madness to go ahead and decide anything at all.

Alan Duncan, aka Hunky Dunky, the diminutive Shadow

Leader of the House, raised himself up on his tiny tiptoes: "We seem to be treading rapidly into realms of complete and utter lunacy." Sir Patrick Cormack, the grand old parliamentarian himself, stood up. "It would seem that this is ..." A voice behind him barked: "A car crash!" Sir Patrick demurred, but agreed that it was inconsistent. Sir George announced that holding the votes was "standing logic on its head". He said: "Rather than come up with quick answers, we should come up with the right answers." "There are no right answers," harrumphed Ken Purchase, a Labour MP.

Right or wrong, Harriet won all her votes. It was exhausting.

6 May

MPs conduct an organised drool

The government had lost the Gurkha vote but, as it wasn't binding, they had agreed only to review their policy. But then Joanna Lumley appeared before the Home Affairs Select Committee, purring like a cat, and everything changed.

The voice was bewitching, the manner beguiling. Joanna Lumley leant forward, looking directly into the eyes of Keith Vaz, chairman of the Home Affairs Select Committee, as he asked her if she had tried to meet the Prime Minister over the Gurkha issue.

In a voice that was so husky with hurt we could hear the bruises, Ms Lumley said: "I wrote to the Prime Minister three times — and my letters haven't been acknowledged." Mr Vaz, who worships celebrity, looked shocked, for he can imagine no circumstance where he would have ignored even a sentence from such a wonderful (and wonderfully famous) creature.

"Do you think such a meeting would have been helpful?" Now it was Ms Lumley's turn to look shocked. "Yes!" she said with a whoosh of intense breathiness that seemed, like an oriental perfume, replete with meanings: yearning, yes, but also regret and a glancing remembrance of what might have been.

My, but it was a performance.

The MPs adored her. It wasn't so much a hearing as an organised drool. Her demeanour was faultless. As the woman who has just defeated the Government, she could have been triumphant and superior. Instead she was humble and gracious.

She had sat in the audience, surrounded by Gurkhas, throughout the painfully defensive testimony of Phil Woolas, the Immigration Minister, still trotting out the penny-pinching arguments that lost him the vote last week. "I may be between a rock and a hard place but I'm not stupid!" he said. No one agreed.

Ms Lumley glided to her seat, an elegant silver kukri brooch on the lapel of her black trouser suit. Her voice was calm. Yes, she had been jubilant but now, "to my shock", she had just heard that the entry-clearance officials in Delhi were still operating on the old rules. "I had understood it was to be discontinued at once," she said. I yearned for dramatically jerky incidental music.

MPs tried to question her but, what with all the drooling, the questions were rather wet. At one point Ms Lumley said to Patrick Mercer, a Tory MP, who hadn't been listening to her answer: "I can see from your face, I'm mumbling."

Mr Mercer looked utterly stricken and began to babble, literally babble, about his "mumbling face".

So what was the next phase of the campaign? "I have been set back slightly," she noted. "I don't know what I have to do. We've gone to the High Court. We've gone to the press. We've gone to the people and we've gone to Parliament. If that's not enough, who do we go to? All of those people have backed the Gurkhas but somehow the rules have not yet been changed."

She was just this side of beseeching. "So who do we go to next? The Royal Family are not allowed to be included, though I personally had a letter of support." At the words "Royal Family" the journalists jumped.

This was news! I had a vision of Liz and Phil, watching the Parliament Channel, cheering as Phil waved his kukri "I don't understand democracy", said Ms Lumley, "if this is not what democracy is." MPs rushed to her aid, I marvelled at her skill. As someone once would have said: "Darling, you were fabulous, absolutely."

8 May
Absolutely Ludicrous!

This was the day when I began to wonder if Joanna Lumley was, actually, running the Government. The entire event had the feel of a Marx Brothers comedy routine.

It was day three of the new Westminster soap opera Absolutely Ludicrous.

Actually I did not think it could get more ludicrous but I was wrong. It could and it did. It is great TV though, perhaps, not the best way to run a government.

It began, as all the best plots do, with a chance meeting on the stairs. These ones were at BBC Westminster. It was 4 pm and our heroine, plucky, gorgeous, pouting Joanna Lumley, was on her way to her daily Gurkha press conference.

The day before Joanna had been ecstatic after a thrilling

meeting with the Prime Minister. Now she was furious because the Government had backtracked. Her nemesis, Phil Woolas (or Phoney Phil as the viewers call him), was already at BBC Westminster, appearing on air to rebut the story that Joanna had not yet told us. (I hope you are keeping up. This is like The Wire but for grown-ups).

Someone spotted Joanna and told her what Phil was up to. Joanna promptly marched into the BBC studio — yes, into the very heart of government — to watch him live, in person, on air.

"I'd love to meet him," said Joanna as she watched. Journalists stared at her for, frankly, no one had ever said this before about Phoney Phil and it seemed too incredible even for Absolutely Ludicrous.

But Joanna insisted it was true. When Phil went off air (though, of course, he never really is), he was enthralled to see Joanna. It was policy at first sight, apparently, and they eloped to a BBC meeting room. I only believe this because, of course, I have seen the pictures.

Meanwhile, below the BBC offices, in the Atrium Restaurant, the hacks who had gathered for Joanna's press conference were getting restless. "They are having a meeting — in my office!" cried BBC man James Landale, on air, pointing up. Then a cry went out from the hacks. Joanna was here! And she was with Phil! The happy couple descended the stairs to the press conference, surrounded by lawyers and cameras and microphones.

"Is this a shotgun wedding?" demanded one journo. Joanna looked demure, Phil proud. He'd had a haircut since yesterday's episode.

They stood on the camera marks. "I have Mr Woolas with me," breathed Joanna who turned away from him and looked down at her left foot as if searching for a handbag.

"Where are you ...?" She turned to her right and found him, grinning like a mad man.

Phil explained his latest ludicrous policy twist which is, basically, this: yes, five Gurkhas had been refused entry but that did not mean they had been refused entry.

Joanna watched, her kohl-rimmed eyes never straying from Phil's face. (God, she's a good actress.) She said, breathily, that she felt reassured. Phil beamed.

Joanna told us about her feelings. "I know I've been accused of being emotional but that's because I'm an actress and a woman and we are always accused of being emotional, of which I am rather proud. You must have emotions: that's our only way of moral guidance."

At the words moral guidance Phil looked a bit lost. Joanna said that she had been up until midnight the night before writing a private letter to the Prime Minister. She had awoken to betrayal but now, after meeting Mr Woolas, she had hope again.

So what was next? "I'm going to ask her to dinner," said Phil, on air, obviously. Joanna looked stunned. The camera faded and the policy, at least for now, went once more into the dark.

12 May

A bad day for Neanderthal Man

When the Telegraph *began its expose on MPs expenses, MPs were furious, not at themselves of course, but at the dastardly media. This was the day that the Speaker, Michael Martin, let rip. His temper tantrum would lead, eventually, to his downfall.*

Petty. Vindictive. Hurt. Defensive. That was Michael Martin, the Speaker of the Commons, yesterday. "I know I'm in a bit of a bad mood," he allowed afterwards. Bad mood? It was like watching a temper tantrum by a Neanderthal who'd had his club taken away. His attire didn't help: at times, as the buffoon black robe ballooned away, he resembled an enraged parachute.

It all started so well too. Mr Martin arose from his throne chair to say that he was going — shock, horror — to hold a meeting on the subject of expenses. MPs, including Jacqui "Bathplug" Smith, nodded.

Barbara Follett, the millionaire Labour MP whom we now know had charged us £25,000 for home security, was hiding behind his chair. She was alone, without even one bodyguard, and I wondered at her bravery.

But trouble loomed in the trim form of Labour maverick Kate Hoey, swathed in a fuchsia scarf the size of Wales. She didn't think that the police should be called in to find whoever had leaked the information to the Telegraph: "Isn't it an awful waste of resources? Will the public not feel, whatever it's meant to be, to be a way of hiding ..."

Mr Martin interrupted. "I listen to you often when I turn on the TV at midnight when I hear your public utterances and your pearls of wisdom on Sky News. It's easy to talk then." He sounded jealous. I noted Ms Hoey was actually wearing pearls. I had a vision of Mr Speaker at midnight, wearing a Wee Willy Winkie hat, throwing a buckled slipper at his TV set. Now he pointed a pudgy finger at Ms Hoey and let rip.

The leaker had also revealed signatures, ex-directory numbers and, the ultimate travesty, passwords. "I just say to you, it's easy to say to the press this should not happen!" fumed Mr Speaker. "Some of us in this House have other responsibilities than talking to the press!"

MPs exchanged looks. Now Norman Baker, who has campaigned long and hard on this issue, arose. He was urging the release of more information when Mr Speaker, robes swishing, cut him off. "Another individual member who is keen to say to the press whatever the press wants to hear!" said Mr Speaker, embarking on another rant, the nub of which was that Mr Baker had said in the past that the Commons authorities had done nothing on this. "It's wrong for you to say that!"

MPs just wanted it to end now. Yesterday should have been the Commons at its best, instead we were seeing it at its worst. But things can always disintegrate even further. Thus it proved when the exotic creature that is Patricia Hewitt (yes, she still exists) arose. "We clearly cannot blame the media for the situation we find ourselves in," she said as MPs, who do blame the media and no one else, glared.

Ms Hewitt, oblivious, rabbited on: "Because it is the public who elect us, and pay for us, would you and the commission consider establishing citizen's juries as they are called ..." "Ohhh!" MPs erupted as if Ms Hewitt had suggested heresy.

Ms Hewitt persevered. "One perhaps for each region to consider the matter both of our salaries and of our ..." This brought unrest. You could see MPs thinking: "Consult the voters? Is she mad?" The robed Neanderthal, reunited with his club, boomed: "Order! Order! I think it's clearly time for me to move on ..." That's funny, lots of people say that's exactly what he should do.

13 May
Tories find moats in their eyes

By this time, we'd read quite a lot about the Tory Squirocracy and their moats, manure, mole-catchers and swimming pools. David Cameron, furious, seized the moment to attack his own MPs.

It was an exercise in ritual humiliation. In the Middle Ages, they had the stocks.

Now we have the instant press conference with David Cameron, Action Man, naming and shaming. For once, he didn't seem to be acting. The rage was real, his blue eyes really did flash, the words spat out like cannonballs.

"No more furniture. No more bathplugs. No more barbecues. No more patio heaters," he chanted. "No more of the things that have caused so much unease."

And no more Mr Nice Guy. Dave had began his day with a unhealthy breakfast of pure rage as he read about Tory MPs and their moats, horse manure, mole-catchers and swimming pools. As he read about people who were even richer than he is, claiming for the curlicues that embellish the lives of the Tory Squirocracy, he saw his future as prime minister passing before his eyes.

Something had to be done. For a moment, he may have entertained the idea of buying some stocks (not on exes, obviously) from the Tower. But who needs stocks when you've got the atrium of Portcullis House at Westminster? Yesterday, at noon, it was impossible to miss the Tory MPs on show as they scurried round under the overpriced fig trees. Labour MPs were there too, plotting like mad against the Speaker, who, it has been agreed, must be removed. "We cannot go on like this," a minister said.

For once, though, Tory MPs were too sheepish even to plot and all the fig leaves in the world (and there were thousands in that atrium) could not save them. It was impossible to look at them without seeing their expenses. I spotted Michael Ancram and thought "swimming pool". There was Oliver Letwin ("tennis court") and George Osborne, the man with the £400 taxi ride!

David Willetts approached and, with his watermelon smile, he looked as lit up as, well, a light bulb. I asked after his 25 light bulbs. "I have heard rather a lot of electricity jokes," he said.

No one could quite get over the fact that Douglas Hogg, a Tory relic, owned a real live moat. "I think I'm suffering from moat envy!" one Tory backbencher moaned. This was an update on the Bible — for the mote in his eye was, actually, a moat.

At his instant press conference, Dave smote the moat and all things moat-ish. He said that he was sorry but it was obvious that, actually, he was angry. "I don't care if they were within the rules," he said of the expenses claims, "they were wrong."

He'd had a series of meetings with his Shadow Cabinet. "So Michael Gove will pay back the £7,000 for furniture. Oliver Letwin will pay back the £2,000 for the pipe under his tennis court ..." The list of shame grew like Pinocchio's nose: Andrew Lansley, Alan Duncan, Francis Maude, Chris Grayling. Other items — David Willetts's light bulbs, his own maintenance bill — would also be paid back.

Dave's voice was sharp. "When I read about the swimming pools and moats, I am completely appalled. Most of my colleagues are appalled. People want something done. The fact is today I can actually announce people are WRITING OUT CHEQUES [he said it in capital letters] and handing them back in the House of Commons."

This was a New Dave we were seeing. His sentences were clipped, his anger hot. The easy bonhomie at which he excels was gone. I have to say that he looked like a prime minister.

14 May

Mistakes, manure and hairshirts

As the expenses scandal rumbled on, MPs were divided into those who had paid money back and those who hadn't. It was all starting to smell like, well, manure.

The party is over, the hangover has begun. The Commons was rife with fear, loathing and self-flagellation yesterday.

Labour grandee Tony Wright, always a voice of sanity, said history had seen the Long Parliament, the Rump Parliament and the Addled Parliament. "If we are not careful," he admonished, "we shall finish up with the Moat Parliament or the Manure Parliament."

The Manure Parliament. You must admit it has a certain ring, if not smell, to it. No one laughed. When you are waist-deep in the stuff, shovel in hand, maybe it's not so funny. Besides, MPs, were hurting too much to laugh.

Remorse, like muck, suffused the air. The guiltfest was awesome to behold.

The Speaker, an expert on manure, was in his place. MPs are now divided between those who have written cheques and those who haven't. I saw Tory Michael Gove (£7,000 for furniture) having a word with Hazel Blears (£13,332 for capital gains) near the doors. "My cheque's bigger than yours," Hazel said (or so I imagined). When you are the tiniest MP, these things matter.

Gordon, Dave and Nick all had their hairshirts on. Indeed, as Ann Widdecombe noted, all MPs are in a competition as to whose hairshirt is the hairiest. It was quite something to behold for I, as a feral beast, as all members of the press are considered to be at Westminster, consider myself an expert on all things hairy.

First Gordo showed us his hairshirt which looked a bit mangy. "We must apologise for mistakes," he said. "We must rectify the errors." There was a committee looking into it, as well as a commission, an inquiry and at least one independent body. It has to be said that the Manure Parliament loves quangos.

Dave (£680 for wisteria clearing) said Gordon's hairshirt was as sad as a man with a comb-over. (I paraphrase.) Dave now modelled his shirt, a hoody no less, which looked designer. He wanted MPs to publish their expenses online "in real time".

He wanted to get rid of the communication allowance worth £10,000 a year for every MP. "Isn't this a gigantic waste of money?"

Gordo, frantically patching his shirt with strange bits of fur, said that he'd already saved loads of money for the taxpayer. "I have myself refused the pension that is able to be given to any serving Prime Minister. I have myself refused the London allowance. As far as the communication allowance, it is open to the House to look at all these things."

Dave slapped the dispatch box. "What we want is some leadership to cut some of these costs. You seem to have such a tin ear to these issues. In an age ..."

A Labour voice cried out: "You're a millionaire!"

Dave glowered and tried to look even hairer. Gordon was still shedding bits of fur. The Manure Parliament was looking as bad as it smelt.

Nick Clegg (£80 for phone calls) is leader of the most hirsute party in the Commons and, sure enough, he did not disappoint. He arose to reveal what can only be called a maxihairshirt. On his feet were special hairy sandals. He said that all Lib Dems were going to give back any profit made from their second homes. "We are here to serve, not make a fast buck on the property market."

Gordo, his shirt now looking as patchy as a piebald cat, said that a committee would look into it. Then they all shuffled out, presumably to flagellate themselves with a spiky ball and chain before shuffling up thousands of stone stairs on their knees.

15 May

It was just perfect except for ...

Labour launched their Euro-election campaign in Derbyshire: it was a lovely day in a lovely location. There was only one thing wrong. Yes, it was the politicians.

It felt more like a wedding reception than a Labour election launch as the 120 guests, many dressed as if for church, walked up the sweeping drive. The place was spotless. The grass was, indeed, greener here, in Derbyshire. In fact the turf was so new that it was curling at the edges. Officially, the building wasn't even open yet.

"It's like a luxury hotel," exclaimed one guest, who admitted that the only politician that she really wanted to meet was David Miliband. "He's such an intellectual." I'm afraid Kirk Hallam Technology College is not quite the Ritz, but it must be said that everything was new and unsullied here except the politicians.

Hazel "Flipper" Blears was there, perkier than ever after writing her £13,000 cheque to the taxman. Had it been cashed yet? "I don't know," she chirped as guests fought — yes, actually fought — to have their picture taken with her. "I've given it to them!"

I looked (down) at her in amazement, even as I was dragooned into taking pictures. She didn't know if a cheque that is more than some people's annual wage had been cashed yet? Who says politicians live in a different world? But it's hard to faze, or indeed haze, Hazey. "I'll be out on the doorstep in Salford tomorrow!" she cried. People of Salford, you've been warned: keep the curtains closed.

The Prime Minister arrived with Ed Balls on his arm (they make a cute couple) surrounded by children and, no, I don't mean the Cabinet but real students who seemed almost giddy after having endured the PM's small talk.

There was a reception line. The PM, espying a new victim, boomed: "So what is your favourite subject!" Physics, the lad said. "Physics!" boomed the PM.

The lad nodded. "Are you taking exams?" boomed Gordon. The lad nodded.

Gordon and Ed now pounced on the dinner ladies. "It's your birthday!" boomed Ed (it's scary how much he's like Gordo). "We should have baked you a cake!"

Inside, 11 circular tables, laden with ridiculously healthy fruit platters, had been arranged in a large airy room with blond wooden floors and peachy walls. Every table had a Cabinet Minister. Margaret Beckett was wearing an outfit as red as the trailing geraniums that she wanted us to buy for her £600 hanging baskets.

As is traditional, Gordon gave a speech. I can report that the Prime Minister has once again located his moral compass. He said everyone had the right to expect the highest standards of everybody in public life. (Does he know we'd settle for middling?) The guests looked at him adoringly. No one had said the words "Europe" or "election" yet.

"When mistakes are made," said Gordon, pacing round without notes, opening and closing his arms as if he were playing an air accordion, "we have got to take action." The expenses system was "antiquated", "ancient" and "outdated". For a moment, I thought he was talking about the Labour Party which, we were told in a pre-wedding reception briefing, thinks this election is "hugely challenging", code for nightmare. Gordo's arms were still wheezing away (was he playing a polka?).

"Where disciplinary action is necessary," he said, "it will be taken." Then he said that Elliot Morley, who is accused of claiming £16,000 for a mortgage that didn't exist, had been suspended from the Parliamentary Labour Party. Gordon didn't even pause when he said this. I'm not sure the guests noticed that the PM had just made the news.

They were too busy taking pictures with their mobile phones.

19 May

Assassins stab away with rubber spatulas

The attempt by MPs to remove Speaker Michael Martin reached farcical levels on this day. MPs had tabled a motion of no confidence. Would it be debated? Dream on.

Disorder! Disorder! The moment the Speaker, Michael Martin, finished his statement, his assassins sprang to their feet. His few friends stayed seated. At this moment, the Prime Minister — a living wreck, eyes hollow, mouth slack — slipped out of the chamber, leaving his fellow Scot on his own.

Looking out, seeing only foes, Mr Martin at least picked an enemy he knew well: Gordon Prentice, serial rebel, serious parliamentarian, as irritating as a mosquito, as persistent as an itch. "A motion of no confidence in you, sir, will appear on the order paper tomorrow," intoned Mr Prentice, dagger in hand. "Am I right in thinking it will be debated and voted upon?"

The Speaker, cowardice flashing like a neon sign, dodged the question: "This is not a point of order!"

Mr Prentice, eyes flashing, shouted: "Oh yes it is!"

"Order!" Mr Speaker bumbled on. "Please allow me to ... Order! ... these are matters for debate on an appropriate motion."

But MPs would not be appropriate or brought to order. They, who can barely organise breakfast, are trying to organise a beheading. Actually it is worse than that. They need to get Mr Martin to organise his own beheading for the benefit of the greater good. Mr Martin, as stubborn as our Prime Minister and not nearly as smart, thinks he can survive by stonewalling.

The assassins kept up the pressure with more questions about the beheading debate. "It is not a substantive motion," Mr Martin insisted, for he believes in pedantry with a fierceness mighty to behold. From the bar of the House, the Tory Richard Bacon bellowed: "It IS a substantive motion!"

Oh, who cares, I thought. But Mr Martin does. He ignored the blatant shows of disrespect (as sure a sign as any that he's a goner) and concentrated on the detail.

Now he leant forward, robes billowing, and consulted his bewigged clerk about the Great Substantive Motion Question. The wig whispered back to him: "It's a motion on a remaining order." Mr Speaker, his tongue twisting, announced: "It's a remaining order on the remaining order!"

Is this farce? Is this history? It is certainly hystery (hysterics, but important hysterics). Mr Speaker is like a whale who, his sonar berserk, has found himself trapped on the beach, flopping around desperately. It's hard to watch. He cannot survive without help, it all smells putrid and rubberneckers, career crash tourists, are flocking by.

The assassins spoke one by one, more in sorrow than in anger. The Tory grandee Sir Patrick Cormack pleaded eloquently. Richard Shepherd, who always sounds close to tears, emitted a cry of pain. David Winnick pointed him towards the door.

Flop. Flop. Flop. Finally Mr Speaker called on a friend, the emollient Sir Stuart Bell. "The majority of this House will fully support the statement you made today," soothed Sir Stuart to shouts of dismay. He heaped praise on the Speaker's statement, which had put forward the brilliant idea that the expenses scandal can be fixed by yet another meeting. "This House should calm itself down," mollified Sir Stuart. "It should have a period of reflection and support you ..."

The encomium was cut short by rebellious shouts. "What world is he living in!" cried one MP. Why, Westminster, of course.

20 May

Pass the sickbag as Mr Speaker goes

The Speaker, disgraced and under siege, had let it be known he would be resigning. In an instant he went from pariah to a paragon of virtue. It was hard to watch.

"S-P-E-E-E-A-K-E-R-R-R!" The tenor's elongated singsong rippled into the ornate Central Lobby just before 2.30 pm as the man himself hove into view, preceded by someone dressed as a penguin and the flame-haired Serjeant of Arms cradling the golden Mace.

Michael Martin, disgraced only the day before, now restored to full pomposity by the act of killing himself, looked almost beatific as he walked, black robes swaying, at a stately pace. His lace-necked trainbearer tripped behind in his slipstream. "Hats off, Strangers!" shouted a policeman as the Speaker's conga processed past the 200 people — tourists, rubberneckers, staff — gathered beneath the huge chandelier. What hats there were stayed put.

Now the procession veered right, trainbearer braking slightly, parading past a line of MPs who promptly burst into applause for the man they'd so recently tried to kill.

Hypocrisy? Well, if you must. But MPs, who love tribalism even more than flat-screen televisions, were just relieved that normal order had been restored. The chamber has probably never been so full for daily prayers, from which the press are barred (for obvious reasons). Thus we journalists filed in just in time to see the old albatross totter to his feet. His soft Glaswegian voice began to susurrate.

Thirty-three seconds. That's how long it took to kill himself. I must say it's about his optimum time for speaking. He said he would "relinquish" — there was feeling in that word — his job on June 21.

"That is all I have to say on this matter," he said. "Order!" MPs deflated visibly. Many had come armed with paeans of praise for they had to slake their guilty consciences. But Mr Martin, bruised and battered, was not giving them that pleasure yesterday. So instead, MPs, as desperate as puppies to show their rediscovered love, walked up to his throne chair to pay their respects. It was like The Godfather except more sinister.

Gordon Brown, chief assassin, was first to shake Mr Martin's hand. It was a brisk exchange of palms. Then came shameless Hazey Blears. Harriet Harman reached out (share the love!) and held his hand in hers. How he must have wanted to snatch it back or, perhaps, slip a frog down the arm of his voluminous robe into her palm.

A queue formed on the Labour side — a crocodile of crocodile tears, at least for some. Ruth Kelly, who knows a thing or two about resignations, squeezed his arm. The Tory Nicholas Soames, a battleship made flesh, smothered his hand in his. This hand sandwich went on for so long I feared an elopement.

As the Adoration of the Speaker continued (I do hope a painting will be commissioned), Mr Martin's face lit up. Even the sudden presence by his side of Dame Gerald Kaufman, wearing total beige with a test-pattern tie, could not darken his mood. At 3.27 pm he disembarked from his chair, with the help of lieges, pitching himself into the several new embraces.

He re-emerged at 7.30 pm, halo clearly visible, to give a statement on expenses. At the end MPs burst into applause, a truly sickbag moment by any standards, even theirs.

21 May

Reputation! Reputation! Reputation!

Shakespeare himself was brought in to witness the horrors that had befallen two peers in the "cash for amendments" scandal. How he would have laughed.

The angst! The hand-wringing! The sheer agony of it all was wondrous to behold. For two hours yesterday the Lords debated whether to suspend two peers for six months over the "cash for amendments" scandal. They saw this as monumental, life-changing, a defining moment in the history of this Sceptred Isle.

"I urge this House to seize the moment!" exhorted Baroness Royall of Blaisdon, the Lord President, so intense and so thin that she resembled a proselytising, red-haired praying mantis.

First she told us of the pain caused. "I've had peers come to me and tell me what at times this has meant: being shouted at in the street, their spouses reluctant to go to their local communities because of what people were saying." Peers nodded, though I think most people would consider this normal life.

"Shakespeare, of course, has the definitive word," she announced, though I wondered if Shakespeare would want to be dragged into it for fear of being shouted at in the street. "Cassio, Othello's loyal aide, catches the issue precisely when he tries to explain to the villainous Iago who has manoeuvred to discredit him, what loss he has endured. 'Reputation, reputation, reputation. Oh I have lost my reputation! I have lost the immortal part of myself and what remains is bestial'."

I looked out on the red benches. They looked about as bestial as aged pussycats napping on a bed. Neither of the two peers — Lords Truscott and Taylor of Blackburn — was there. Indeed, of the original four accused, only Lord Snape, moustache twitching, had the guts to attend. He had been found guilty only of inappropriate conduct and will have to make a personal statement. It is, as I am sure Shakespeare would agree when Lady Royall mentions it to him, a cruel punishment.

Most of the debate centred on whether the Lords had the power to suspend a peer. Not expel, mind you, suspend. The Attorney-General, Baroness Scotland of Asthal, sitting on the front bench, resplendent in regal purple, did not think it did.

The former Lord Chancellor Lord Mackay of Clashfern had disagreed.

Everyone agreed with Lord Mackay. Legal luminaries, as common as crabgrass in the Lords, jumped up to explain why.

I feared what Cassio would say about Lady Scotland's reputation. She sat, as serene as a reflecting pool, until finally she felt stirred to defend her honour.

"This is a vexed matter which has tested the House on a number of occasions since 1642," she said. Many members looked dreamy, for they remember it well.

"The Republic was in being, Cromwell was in position and two loyalists Lords were suspended because they went to the King as opposed to coming to this Parliament."

I wondered, briefly, if those Lords had been shouted at in the street (or, perhaps, beheaded, as was the fashion of the day). The Lady, very grave now, admonished her peers: "I simply say: be cautious!" Then they did the dastardly deed. History had been made. Shakespeare would approve, I'm sure.

22 May

Joanna wins the day! Ayo Gorkhali!

It was La Lumley who announced, breathlessly of course, the official change in the government's Gurkha policy. Then Jacqui "Bathplug" Smith had a go too.

The Gurkha policy was announced first, as our updated constitution demands, to Joanna Lumley in person by the Prime Minister. "I did as I promised," he whispered, head ducking like a lovestruck schoolboy, when they met at No 10 at 8.45 am. La

Lumley smiled at him indulgently, holding his eyes with hers as the camera rolled.

Mr Brown leant forward eagerly, blushing as he remembered their last meeting when he had cast himself on the ground before her and told her to rewrite the Gurkha policy as she saw fit. "How brave you are," she had said, as he stared at her perfect feet.

Now Joanna emerged glowing with happiness, drawn like a magnet to the cameras outside in Downing Street. "Can we just say something, which is that we aren't really allowed to say anything!" She paused for a moment to look ecstatic. "The meeting was extremely positive." She struggled to stop herself saying more — and failed. "We've got to wait for Jacqui Smith's announcement at 12.30 pm, but we feel ..." she paused to glow for a long, tantalising moment — "outstandingly optimistic!"

I wondered if, this one time, Joanna could act as Home Secretary. After all, she seemed to be in charge. But now La Lumley was telling us, once again, how she couldn't talk. "Today's the first time in my life I can't have words, I mustn't say them, but it was superb! A superb meeting!"

Golly, golly, gosh! And as Joanna decreed so it was. At 12.30 pm Jacqui "Bathplug" Smith, looking a bit deflated these days, it must be said, made a statement. Irritatingly, she talked mostly about the Gurkhas and not Joanna. MPs gazed longingly up to the balcony, where their heroine would normally be sitting. Yesterday, though, she wasn't watching for she was outside, across the road, giving a rolling press conference. Her blonde hair flowed in the gentle wind as she stood with the Gurkhas, holding, in her perfect hand, a radio blaring out Jacqui Smith's words.

When the announcement came, Joanna and her band of brothers punched the air. "AYAGUKANAA!" they screamed. Later,

I learnt this was "Ayo Gorkhali!", or "Here come the Gurkhas!" (Surely that should be updated to: "Ayo Joanna Lumley!"). In the boring old Commons MPs jumped up to heap praise on Joanna, as they now call her. Tory MP Iain Duncan Smith said that, in future, ministers should find better chat-up lines for Joanna. Lembit Opik said the people of Montgomeryshire had been united in support of Ms Lumley. A Labour MP spoke of his fears for soldiers who had fought in Kenya, Singapore, Malaysia. "They never had a Joanna Lumley," he said sadly. MPs were silent, as they digested this terrible fact.

The moment the statement was over, there was a stampede out of the Commons to be nearer the sainted one. The Gurkhas, who could not stop smiling, held up a hand-made sign glued to a bit of cardboard that said: "Thank You Mr Gordon Brown, From All the Gurkhas". Joanna, surrounded by soldiers, was doing rolling interviews interspersed with screams of "Aayo Gurkhali!" She kept calling the Prime Minister brave. Later his spokesman was asked if Mr Brown thought Ms Lumley should be made a Dame. "He is a great admirer of her campaigning skills," said the spokesman, also blushing. Surely it is only a matter of time before she becomes Baroness Lumley of Absolutely Fabulous.

23 May

I'm Dave and I'm very, very sorry

When it came to the subject of MPs expenses, David Cameron had adopted a masochism strategy. Here he met his constituents, grovelling like a pro.

To Witney, in deepest Oxfordshire, to see David Cameron face his constituents. The showdown was set for high noon at the Corn Exchange. The crowd was very Middle England. Think WI, garden centre, Waitrose shoppers. I haven't seen so many men in V-neck jumpers in ages. If this was going to be a lynching, it was going to be a genteel one.

Dave arrived saying sorry. Sorry, sorry, sorry. My but he was contrite. Grovel, grovel, grovel. He wasn't just on the naughty step, he'd brought his own naughty step, labelled, so everyone could see it. It was a bit like a Politicians Anonymous outreach meeting. "Hi I'm Dave and I'm a politician!" he cried (or so I imagined) as he stood next to the stage, looking up at a sea of pastel colours and hair rinse.

It wasn't so much Dave Unplugged as Dave Confidential. He began by confessing all about his mortgage interest.

"Even though I am relatively well off, I still claim," he said, looking a bit furtive. I loved that "relatively". It is said that he and his wife are worth £30 million. (Dave, when asked about that, later, managed to look a bit shocked and said: "If so, I'd love to know what she's done with it!" The crowd laughed. The whole incident, with that graceful sidestep laced with charm, was very Tony Blair.) But I digress. Back in 2001, Dave took out a "quite big" mortgage of £350,000. Again, I liked that "quite big". His mortgage interest was £1,700 a month. The pastel people leaned forward, for this was pure financial voyeurism.

In 2007 Dave managed to pay off £100,000 (as you do). He also began to claim for utilities. But no moats. "And no duck houses!" said a voter. "No duck houses!" trilled Dave, laughing a bit too hard. He told us all about the wisteria bill. It was too much information. As he explained the intricacies of his chimney venting, I felt a desire to take a nap.

The room, with its 200 people, was beginning to steam. Dave ripped off his city-slicker jacket (also a classic Tony Blair gesture). He said he knew people were angry and then, as if to prove how angry he was, he said UKIP didn't know their "arse from their elbow". The moment he said "arse" he looked almost pleased. "And we are on TV!" he cried. But then Dave is always on TV, I think.

The crowd let rip in a very quiet way, more the sound of a zipper than a thunderclap but a noise nonetheless. They hated the greed, the Speaker, the sheer corruption of it all. Dave listened hard and kept saying how much he loved being their MP. I could see his grovel strategy was working: the pastel people hated politicians in general, but not Dave in particular.

But they had no sympathy. "It is said that some MPs are suffering from depression and talking about suicide," said one woman with a Minnie Mouse voice. "Well, we would really, really like to see them hanging from the lampposts!" As I said, a very genteel lynching. There will be hanging baskets of flowers on those lampposts too.

Dave also has no sympathy (as his party is finding out). "I agree that MPs having depression is not an issue," he said. "They should be depressed about what's happened." Then he grovelled some more.

— ENDS SPRING —

THE SUMMER OF DESPAIR

Could it get worse? Of course it could! Summer began with an election disaster for Labour, a series of Cabinet resignations and a make-or-break reshuffle. There were many who thought Gordon could not survive the shock betrayal of the young and thrusting James Purnell. Then there was the bizarre resignation of Little Hazel Blears with her "Rocking the Boat" badge. But Gordon staggered on (and on). By the end of the summer, we had a new Speaker, Peter Mandelson was in charge of the universe and Sirallun had become Lord Sugarpuff. And then, of course, there was Afghanistan…

2 June

Yo Blair! He's back, for just a minute

Tony Blair, for it is he, swept into Westminster to give us an update on Middle East peace. It was hard not to compare him with Gordon Brown who was sounding more discombobulated by the day

He's back and this time he's got the tan just right. Tony Blair, so often orange, now the perfect shade of light brown, swept by us in the corridor on his way into the Foreign Affairs committee, as sleek as an expensive car. His entourage of six flowed behind, riding his wake. Even his hangers-on have good tans now.

I felt an unexpected wave of nostalgia. Yo Blair, I thought, as he slipped into his chair, engine purring, and took off his navy jacket to reveal the trademark whiter-than-white shirt, iron creases visible.

He sat still, eyes guarded but alert as they slipped over the various newly discredited MPs before him (they included "Mr Manure", David Heathcoat-Amory). I do hope Gordon was taking time out of his manic radio and television interview schedule to watch the master at work. The PM seems to be all over the place, more "Yo-yo Brown" than anything else. Hours before, on the Today programme, when asked how much trouble he was in, Mr Brown said: "I've got to get on with the job. You know every morning I get up ..." There was a pause during which I reflected how weird this sounded. "... and I look obviously at what people have to say."

I like that "obviously". Things must be very bad indeed because Mr Blair did not mention the war once yesterday. (Not the Iraq war, obviously, as Mr Brown would say, but the far more damaging expenses war.) There was no typically Blair wry aside about second homes. Indeed he never even said the word "brown" which, given the centrality of the tan issue, is quite a feat. The MPs also did not mention the war. For a glorious two hours, it was as if the expenses crisis did not exist. Mr Blair, or Tony as MPs called him, was in world statesman mode, explaining his Middle East envoy role.

Mr Blair had nothing new to say and he said it brilliantly. He sat, hands held out in front of him, tanned fingers tapping together in their own private Morse code. He is calmer and trimmer these days with the patina of the rich. Maybe it's the lack of eyebags but he looks, skin taunt over cheekbones, aerodynamic.

I thought of poor Gordon, as rumpled as a Shar-Pei. Mr Blair, who always speaks with bullet points in mind, has the gift of making something complicated, such as Middle East peace, sound understandable. Gordon takes something easy, such as his Chancellor's expenses, and makes it sound unfathomable. There are more than homes being flipped here: by the end of the day Yo-yo Brown had changed his answers so often I felt seasick.

Back in the calm waters of the committee room, Mr Blair, unruffled, unflipped, was telling us about his little chats with Barack Obama. He and Barack were both optimists. June was going to be a vital month. Did he ever talk to Iran? "I occasionally meet the Iranians," he said airily, "but more by chance than by design." He made it sound as random as a taxi driver ("I had that Mr Ahmadinejad in the back of my cab ..."). When it was over, Labour MPs queued up to pay their respects to Mr Blair, still glowing like a lava lamp. I bet they wonder why they ever got rid of him.

3 June

Jacqui Smith's non-leaving leaving do.

We all knew that Jacqui Smith was leaving her job to spend more time with her (second) home. She knew she was leaving. So why was she pretending otherwise?

What a mess. The Home Secretary made her last appearance in the Commons yesterday while pretending it was nothing of the kind. The whole ghostly event was like some sort of non-leaving leaving do. If it sounds mad, that's because it was. But then a box of frogs would be saner than Westminster at the moment.

The news broke at lunchtime that Jacqui Smith was quitting the Cabinet to spend more time in her (second) home. She had made no comment when she arrived in the Commons for the debate on her latest Immigration Bill in an outfit as black and white as a piano keyboard. I thought the rumour must be true as one of her friends was jumping round, giving her an excited thumbs-up.

It soon became clear that Ms Smith was going to pretend that her resignation hadn't happened. "I beg to move that the Bill be read," she began mechanically when a volcanic shout erupted from the Tory benches. "WHY!" cried Desmond Swayne, a flamboyant Tory whose flowing white locks seemed to be in a tidal state. Was he referring to her non-resignation resignation? Or the Bill? Ms Smith's lips tightened into a grim line reminiscent of a prison guard. She waxed lyrical about her wondrous immigration system. Mr Swayne, who seemed to be in the grip of political Tourette syndrome, kept barking his disapproval. "That's a good lunch," shouted a Labour MP at him. Mr Swayne did not sway in response but I got the feeling he could have.

The Speaker (who's also resigned but at least it's official) intervened.

Ms Smith's eyes flicked over Mr Swayne. "The honourable gentleman's had lunch but he didn't have coffee!" This got a laugh, not least from Mr Swayne.

It was the finest moment of her non-resignation resignation but then Ms Smith is always at her best when impersonating a barmaid. Then she got on with the business of impersonating the Home Secretary, talking about her future plans as if she had a future. It was, truly, surreal. She told us that, next on her agenda, she wanted to introduce a points-based citizenship system. This had her backbenchers jumping around like mad. I marvelled at her.

This wasn't really a case of the emperor having no clothes but much like the clothes having no emperor. She sat down, having thoroughly confused everyone in the Chamber.

It was left to Chris Grayling, her Conservative shadow, to say the unsayable: "It's probably appropriate to begin my remarks this afternoon by marking what now appears to be certainly the Home Secretary's final appearance at the dispatch box."

He looked over at her for confirmation. Her face was blank, her lips once again frog-marched into that grim little line. He noted that she was Britain's first female Home Secretary. At this Ms Smith looked even more miserable.

As tributes go, it was grudging and, as such, that rarest thing in politics, entirely authentic. "I would like to congratulate her on her decision to pre-announce the reshuffle!" Mr Grayling chortled, adding that this must have prompted a few mobile phones to be thrown in Downing Street.

"But I would congratulate you for your achievements in being Britain's first woman Home Secretary," he said clumsily, repeating himself already.

At the word "achievements", Ms Smith allowed herself a tiny smile. Then she got up and left, still pretending she wasn't leaving at all.

4 June

Gordon, grin attached, staggers on

It was a day of pure government chaos. Reshuffle rumours were rife. Jacqui Smith let it be known she was to go and Hazel Blears resigned as Communities Secretary — the day before the local elections. Later she arrived back home wearing a badge that said: "Rocking the boat". But at Prime Minister's Questions, the ship seemed to be capsizing…

Gordon Brown entered the Chamber not so much a dead man walking as a dead man staggering. He had just been shot by Little Hazel Blears. Who knew she had it in her?

Actually, those pictures of her in baby-sized motorcycle leathers astride her toy bike should have told us that she had a dark side. She may be a munchkin but she is a munchkin who can shoot. Mr Brown smiled as he staggered, as you do when you have lost four ministers in 24 hours. When they saw him Labour MPs let rip with a raggedy cheer. As propaganda goes, it was ropey stuff. As he heard it, Gordon's horror-movie stick-on grin widened.

It is a curious fact that the worse things get the happier the Prime Minister seems. As you may recall he was almost ecstatic when the economy was in freefall. Now, bodies strewn around him, his Cabinet openly feuding, his body so riddled with bullet holes that he resembles a piece of Swiss cheese, he seemed to be bursting with bonhomie.

David Cameron, who had expected a thundercloud but faced a ray of sunshine, growled out a question about Cabinet chaos.

Gordon went all dreamy. "The first thing the House would want to do is acknowledge the great work that has been done by both the Home Secretary and the Community Secretary," he enthused.

"Hear, hear!" cried a few Labour MPs (they must be being paid) as the Tories yelped. Gordon heaped praise on Jacqui "Bathplug" Smith, who had rushed in from the television studios to sit on the front bench for the last time. She had tackled terrorism. She had brought crime down. He did not mention her fight against porn.

Dave looked exasperated. "The Prime Minister is in denial," he said, which made Gordon beam more. So, Dave asked, if these people were so great why were they leaving? "The minister in charge of local government is resigning the day before the local elections. Isn't that a direct challenge to your authority?"

Gordon looked thrilled and said that he wanted to pay tribute to Hazel. "She has sponsored urban regenerations in shopping centres in our country," he said, going all soppy as he thought of plucky Little Hazie healing our nation's neighbourhoods.

Oh dear. The PM may not need to go to the Priory yet but, I've got to say it, this was odd behaviour. I have heard of hugging your enemies close but this was love-bombing. The rats were leaving the sinking ship and Mr Brown was giving them vermin-sized medals for doing so. Later, when it emerged that Hazel was about to be sacked, it stank even more.

On the front bench all the Cabinet ministers looked stressed (assassination is hard work after all) and Alistair Darling the worst of all. Even his eyebrows looked deflated. Dave turned his attention to whether the Prime Minister had faith in Mr Darling. Would the Chancellor still be in post in a week?

The PM dosed Mr Darling with a water-cannon of praise. "Let me say what this Chancellor is achieving! This Chancellor is leading the rest of the world!"

Oh dear, that sounds very worrying indeed. Soon, perhaps, the only action that Mr Darling will be taking is redundancy. Politics is cruel.

5 June

When in doubt, blame the women

Election day dawned and Westminster was deserted, rumours of resignations of one kind or another (almost all of them female including, now, Caroline Flint, portrayed as a virtual femme fatale in the media) rolling round like tumbleweeds.

I blame the women, of course. If you look, they are everywhere. Take yesterday. It began with the tantalising hint of another resignation when Ed Miliband, the brother without the fruit fetish, was not on the front bench for his departmental questions.

"Has he resigned?" shouted the Tories.

Joan Ruddock, a rogue female minister, jumped up to answer. I marvelled that she had survived, for Ms Ruddock is a member of the notorious para-parliamentary organisation the Volupts, who have wreaked such havoc on the Government this week. Now she simpered, in the way that treacherous females can, that Mr Miliband's partner, Justine, had just given birth.

This meant that Ed had abandoned his Government to take paternity leave. Aha, I thought, I knew there would be a woman behind this somehow.

Greg Clark, the Shadow Energy and Climate Change Secretary, also saw the connection. "I'm lost in admiration for the meticulousness of Ed's planning that he can provide himself with an excuse to go to ground this weekend."

Forget the weekend. Baby, they're gone. For Labour MPs this was Thank God It's Thursday week. Outside Parliament, on College Green, cameras stood, unused. The Mary Celeste (another female) has seen busier days. In politics, as in airports, there is a great deal of something called "hurry up to wait". You rush to get somewhere only to wait hours for an event. This was a hurry-up-to-wait day in our constitutional crisis.

But, in the same way that the sky turns green before a tornado, there were signs of the reshuffle to come. Sir Alan Sugar arrived via the back door at No 10, prompting lots of "You're fired!" jokes. The few Labour MPs around were clinging to their BlackBerrys like lifeboats, desperately trying to maintain their wi-fi connection long enough to mount Britain's first e-mail beheading.

Harriet Harman, a woman and a founding member of the Volupts to boot, was in the chamber, pretending that Labour MPs were out campaigning. The Tories, mob-handed, didn't believe her. I was relieved to see that Harriet was not wearing her killer stilettos. The Government was safe for one more day. There was a moment, watching her, when you could almost feel how fragile it all was. A Lib Dem had noted that next week there would be a debate on whether to dissolve Parliament. Would the Prime Minister be opening that?

Harriet looked wistful and, for a moment, lost in thought (I'm giving her the benefit of the doubt). "It's a matter for the

Government," she said distractedly.

"You ARE the Government," shouted the Lib Dem.

This jolted her. "Quite so," she whispered. "Quite so."

Soon even she had fled the chamber, taking with her the one remaining Labour backbencher (Sir Peter Soulsby, arise, you've done your time). This left Ian Pearson, the Economic Secretary and the worst speech-maker in the Government, to open the debate on The Economy: Supporting Business. Behind him there were no — I counted twice just to be sure — backbenchers.

Greg Hands, for the Tories, said that this was incredible not least because the debate could be historic, the last to take place with Alistair Darling as Chancellor. "This could be how it all ended," he noted, "a dead-end debate slot on European election day with virtually nobody here to witness the end to it all. The Chancellor would be like a modern-day Eleanor Rigby. Surely Britain deserves better than this."

Eleanor Rigby. She's a woman. I rest my case.

6 June

What next ... a karaoke "I did it my way"?

This was the day after the nightmare before. The evening before, James Purnell, the young ambitious Blairite with the dodgy sideburns, had resigned dramatically, telling Gordon Brown to "stand aside". Would there be a coup? The day was eerily quiet until the PM gave a snap press conference.

Knackered. Nervous. Determined. A bit punch-drunk. The man who many thought wouldn't last the day as our Prime Minister emerged at 4.45 pm yesterday, at his reshuffle press conference, with that strange smile plastered to his face.

"I'm here to be totally candid, to accept my responsibility and to set out what I intend to do," he announced.

Well, if that is candid, then I'd hate to see shifty. There were even a few blatant porkies in there, such as when he claimed he never, ever wanted to move Alistair Darling as Chancellor. To that, many would say just one word: "Balls."

So he's taking responsibility but, then, as he explained, it's not his fault. It's a global crisis. It's an expenses' crisis. He's the answer, not the problem. His face had a strange patina and at times he rocked to and fro, his arms flapping. But then, I reminded myself, he'd been in the bunker for way too long.

His tie was bright purple, his rhetoric equally so. At times he appeared to be speaking in some sort of haiku-inspired verse.

"*I have faith in doing my duty.*

"*This is who I am.*

"*I believe in never walking away.*

"*This is what I stand for.*

"*I have the determination ...*

"*This is what I am doing!*"

I halfway expected him to grab a microphone and start booming out My Way. Actually, in addition to Frank Sinatra, he seemed to be channelling Churchill (it is the eve of D-Day after all). "Yes, it was a tough night. But we fight on for what we believe. I will not waver. I will not walk away. I will get on with the job. And I will finish the work!" I could see James Purnell hurling his shoe at the television.

Watching Gordon perform, I was amazed that anyone ever thought he'd leave: the man would nail himself to No 10 if he had to. Indeed, his belief in himself is a bit Messianic. It soon became clear he will stop at nothing. He's even taking his new Defence Secretary, Bob Ainsworth, to today's D-Day events. The Queen can't go, but Boring Bob can. Surely those soldiers have suffered enough already.

Outside Downing Street, it had been a duck of a day, calm on the surface, frantically paddling below. The political paparazzi who live there, across from that gleaming black door, had nothing to do other than watch the begonias grow and interview the delicate flower that is Peter Mandelson, who has, surprise, surprise, organised a promotion for himself. (The acronym for his new department is D'Bis, pronounced The Biz.) News of the reshuffle came in dribs and drabs through the rolling news channels. Resignations and appointments merged into one. Hain is back, Hutton and Hoon out. (Forget the number of women, what about the number of Hs in the Cabinet?) And let's not forget Sirallun who will, presumably, soon be Lord Sugarpuff.

On the green opposite Parliament, a collection of tents and gazebos (the ones you can buy at B&Q with fake church windows) had sprung up. Here, throughout the day, reshuffle refugees roamed from tent to tent, grazing on soundbites and gossip.

Tourists stopped to stare (as you would). I befriended a group of Danish women wearing plastic see-through rain ponchos taking mobile phone pictures of Siobhain McDonagh, the Labour rebel, dressed in what appeared to be white satin evening-wear. Did they know what this was all about? They nodded. "George Brown is in trouble," said one. I nodded. So he was but, it must be said, not as much as before.

9 June

UKIP triumphs! It's a celebration

The Euro and local government elections were good for the Tories and a disaster for Labour but, for zany little UKIP, they were a stunning success. I watched them crow.

To UKIP's celebratory press conference, where almost everyone looks just this side of bonkers. It's held in the smallest room for rent in Westminster — curtains closed to give it that murky underwater feel — and is crammed with men of a certain age wearing giant purple UKIP rosettes. It's chaotic and crowded, full of TV cameras, wires, photographers, loud voices.

Loudest of all is Nigel Farage, UKIP's leader, chortling, booming, dominating all with an XXL personality. "In 2004 we came third in the Euro elections and they said it was a fluke," he crowed, Euro-tan glowing. "I'm very pleased to sit here and say that UKIP has come second! Of course this time we'll be told it was a fluke again. Although Gary Player, the famous golfer, said, 'It's funny, the more I practise, the luckier I get!'"

It's hard to take UKIP seriously when you are this close to them. I think that, as a party, they should bulk-buy breath mints. As Hazel Blears (RIP) may have said: "UKIP if you want to ..." But as Nige, as I already think of him, points out, the truth is that more people are wanting to.

Nige tells us why it all went wrong in 2004 when Robert Kilroy-Silk, the deeply orange celebrity politician, was in the party. "Let's be frank! We completely blew it in 2004! We blew it because we went into a period of total civil war!" This time, though, it's different. "I don't see those sorts of splits coming. I don't see anybody with an ego quite as big as that." He snorted. "It wouldn't be possible!"

The place was full of unlikely types. Take Nikki Sinclaire, a very tall (reportedly 6ft 4in) lesbian who has just become a UKIP MEP. Well, I say to her, you're on the gravy train now.

"Yes, but I want to get off. I want to pull the cord. I've already started to campaign for my own redundancy!"

Then I meet Lord Dartmouth, hereditary peer and new MEP.

Dartmouth, I ask, like the place?

"Like the author!" cries the UKIP peer Lord Pearson of Rannoch.

The author?

"Barbara Cartland!" cries Lord Pearson.

"She was my grandmother," says Lord Dartmouth.

Then there's David Campbell-Bannerman, MEP and distant relation of the former Liberal PM Sir Henry Campbell-Bannerman (is he the least famous of all PMs?). The family still has Sir Henry's desk which, David reveals, has a drinks cabinet in it. Ah, drink! This has a certain resonance with UKIP for Nige admits to liking a drink or two. I catch him afterwards, immediately after his interview with Lauren Booth, Cherie Blair's half-sister, who now works for the Iranian-owned Press TV. (Sometimes it really is very, very hard to keep up in Westminster.) Nige is smoking a thin cigar that looks dangerously like a cigarillo.

"Smoking!" I cry. Nige says that in Brussels he flouts the smoking law. "In Europe, laws are merely advisory. You can't tell the Greeks in the EU Parliament not to smoke! It just isn't going to work."

So will he be celebrating with a drink or two? I say that I heard that two UKIP MEPs had to be dragged out of the pub for the press conference (it was at 11 am).

"Just the one," corrected a minder.

"And he was only halfway there."

Nige puffed away. "I've got a couple of things to do first. But we will go for a couple. Definitely! And WHY NOT?"

9 June

Gordon's thumping success

Another make-or-break day for Gordon (a much over-used phrase but, this time, true). Labour had had its worst ever election. Many blamed Gordo. MPs said he had to change! He came to tell the Parliamentary Labour Party that he could.

Right on time, Gordon Brown swept down the Committee Corridor at the House of Commons, lined three-deep with journalists. "Hi guys!" No fake smile today. His security men peeled off as he entered Committee Room 14.

Within minutes, we heard the noise — pound, pound, pound. Hands hitting desks. Then the cheers and whistles. The rumble in the political jungle was going for Gordon.

It was a secret meeting: inside politicians were packed like sardines; outside, lobby journalists roamed, utterly clueless.

We could not hear words, only sounds. At 6 pm we had the thumping and then silence. We knew someone was talking, we assumed the Prime Minister but we did not know. T.S. Eliot wrote of a life measured out in coffee spoons. Yesterday, Mr Brown's political life was measured out in thumps.

6 pm: medium thumping.

6.11 pm: mini thumping.

6.18 pm: more mini thumps 6.27 pm: massive thumping. What is "massive thumping"? Think of a thousand rabbits, feet hammering against a wooden floor: a stampede of rabbits. The PM must have quit speaking. He was either safe or MPs and peers had thudded over in a group faint.

At 6.45 pm, peers had to leave to vote. Geoff Hoon escaped

also, using them as camouflage. Seven o'clock came and went; random thumps could be heard. Then, finally, at 7.33 pm, the rabbits burst out, desperate to tell us how united they all were. But then herds usually are.

10 June

Beyond infinity for Prince of Darkness

Lord Mandelson seemed to be the only person who actually benefited from the reshuffle but, until this moment, I had no idea how vast his empire was.

Breaking news! I knew that Baron Mandelson, of Foy in the County of Herefordshire and Hartlepool in the County of Durham, as he is officially called, was grand but, until yesterday, I had no idea just how incredibly important he has become.

For it has been revealed that his new empire is, literally, out of this world.

Mandy had graced the Lords with his presence, post-reshuffle, to explain his giant new department and his ludicrously long list of titles which puts even the Grand Poobah's into the shade.

"Can I congratulate the Lord President of the Council and First Secretary of State on your remarkable accumulation of responsibilities, titles and junior ministers, of whom you can boast no fewer than ten, surely a record," noted Lord Hunt of Wirral, a Tory. "I understand that you have also now added outer space to your portfolio. Your ambition indeed knows no bounds!"

At the words "outer space", Mandy inclined his head graciously. Oh my God, I thought, before realising that God, if there is a Heaven, is now a mere stakeholder in Mandy's empire.

It seems that the reshuffle was one small step for Mandy, one giant leap for mankind. The aliens have no idea what they are in for.

Mandy was magnanimous in victory. "What we have in this new department is indeed a new phoenix that is going to take flight from the merger of two previously excellent departments," he said, his voice silky, his hand stroking the despatch box, "and will be able to extend its reach to outer space and beyond."

And beyond? Lord Hunt attacked the merging of Mandy's business empire with the department for universities and skills. "In the business world there is said to be no such thing as mergers, only takeovers. Do you not agree that it's a shameful and retrograde development that further and higher education have been subsumed in this way, to be judged not worthy even of a single letter in the departmental acronym?" Piffle, said Mandy, or something like that. He insisted that, as a liberal arts graduate (PPE, St Catherine's, Oxford), he could be trusted with the future of our universities as well as our universe.

Various peers wobbled up to announce that they had degrees in dead languages or, in the case of one bishop, dead ideas. As always in the Upper House, peers perked up at the word "dead".

Now Lord Hunt sent them into orbit (oops, another Mandy responsibility) with reference to Sir Alan Sugarpuff. "In a country in need of enterprise, when are we going to meet the so-called enterprise czar? When will the sorcerer's apprentice make his debut?" At the words "sorcerer's apprentice", Mandy threw his head back and barked with laughter.

"Or is he already a falling czar!" cried Lord Hunt, who had the grace to look embarrassed at this appalling pun.

"Ohhhhhh," groaned the peers.

Mandy played along, though, as ever, only for a moment.

"I'm sure the sorcerer's apprentice will be winging his way" (for these words he used his special Prince of Darkness voice, lower and spookier) "towards your lordships' house in due course."

Lords and ladies looked ecstatic. (I feared, though, that in the Upper House his catchphrase would have to be "You're tired".) Mandy looked even more mysterious. As Buzz Lightyear, that toy of toys, would say: "To infinity and beyond!"

16 June

The Speakers who talk too much

In the end, the contest to be Speaker of the House of Commons, which involves living in splendour and wearing silly outfits, attracted 10 MPs. It seemed way too many.

There has never been a Speaker's hustings before and now we know why. At least half of the MPs who want to be Speaker should avoid speaking. Oh they can spew out the words all right. But, for the good of the nation, they should avoid doing so unless for purposes such as to an Insomniacs Anonymous meeting.

There were ten of them. Ten!

Democracy is so tedious at times (something President Ahmadinejad has yet to find out). Indeed, there may have been more MPs running for Speaker than there were MPs listening at the Hansard hustings. With so much hot air, the room was sauna-like. Thankfully, politicians kept their clothes on. Naked views, though, were all on show.

Here, then, are my verdicts:

— John Bercow: most irritating. It's official. Rampaging cows are in the news and, like them, it is clear that Ber-Cows must be avoided too. Sanctimonious didn't even begin to cover the patronising pitch by this bumptious little Tory. His speech was mystifying. "Eight is the Chinese lucky number," he announced, "but nine is the more interesting figure." He told us about nine for a while. Why? Then all became clear. "If I were so fortunate as to be elected Speaker, I would be the youngest holder of the office since 1839!" He is, of course, the favourite.

— Sir George Young: small cycle crash for the bicycling baronet. At one point Margaret Beckett (who, bizarrely, called herself the "healing" candidate) announced she'd voted for Sir George last time. "Good girl!" said Sir George, oozing Eton, though at least he didn't say "gel". He classified himself as among the "great and the good" in the Commons. He also said that people should vote for him because, if he were a horse, he had the longest legs. It made sense to me.

— Parmjit Dhanda: surprisingly good. The young Sikh (at age 37 even younger than rampaging Ber-Cow) is a modernising radical. "People don't want the language of Erskine May," he said, referring to the eponymous Commons handbook. "They want plain blunt English." He wants to hold debates in places such as Sidcup. Take Parliament to the people? It will never catch on.

— The Dulls. I'm not anti-Dull because, who knows, a Dull could be great. Yesterday they included Sir Alan Beith (worthy but Dull), Sir Michael Lord (avuncular but Dull), Mother Beckett (a "healing" Dull) and Sir Alan Haselhurst (crisp but Dull).

— Sir Patrick Cormack: the circular candidate. Plus points for Dame Patrick, as he is sometimes known, include that he says Parliament by pronouncing the "i" and the second "a" with a little vocal wiggle. "I'm not standing merely because someone told me that we needed a rounded figure as Speaker," he said, face beaming like a giant Jaffa cake. At one point he announced: "We must remember our Burke!" Indeed.

— Richard Shepherd: cry baby. Mr Shepherd, who has way too much integrity, made a heartfelt plea but then he always seems on the brink of tears. His speakership would be principled chaos but it would be fun to hear "Order! Order!" with real tears.

— Ann Widdecombe: the commonsense candidate. "Let's just say I'm pretty unique," she began to cries of "hear, hear". She says that she possesses the "vulgar attributes" to connect with the public. If elected, she pledged to shun Have I Got News for You. The best one yesterday, though only a temporary fix.

My vote — and, yes, sketchwriters should get votes — is still up in the air though I am now, officially, against Ber-Cow.

17 June

Shock! Harriet is struck dumb

Amid all the furore at Westminster, the quiet figure of Sir Christopher Kelly, whose inquiry is charged with resolving the MPs' expenses crisis, was getting on with the job. This is the day Harriet came out to play.

Sir Christopher Kelly's inquiry into MPs' expenses is being held in a former church hall and, over the entrance, there is this admonition: "Heal the sick, cleanse the lepers, raise the dead, cast out the demons." It is from the Bible but, actually, it seemed a thoroughly up-to-date assessment of what the British public would like Sir Christopher and his committee to do.

Harriet Harman was the first to appear. As she entered with her entourage of seven, I wondered what category the woman known as Harriet Harperson was in: more demonised than demon, I suppose, although she knows a thing or two about being treated like a leper. She sat facing Sir Christopher and his interrogators on their makeshift horseshoe table that had been covered in blue material as if this were a rather cheap-o wedding reception. It was all tremendously ad hoc and very, very British.

To one side, there was a huge banner that said: "Selflessness. Integrity. Objectivity. Accountability. Openness. Honesty. Leadership." MPs will find that list terrifying, not least because none can be bought on exes. "These values are timeless," intoned Sir Christopher. "If they had been followed more by more MPs over the past few years we would not be in this situation."

Harriet began with an intensely long grovel, saying how far MPs had already come. As to second homes, MPs needed to have a family life. She wasn't in favour of the "Barack Solution". Her voice, tiny and girly in the echoing hall, was hard to hear and I wondered what President Obama had to do with this.

I quickly got the point when Sir Christopher noted the public's favourite idea as to where MPs should be housed during the week was, indeed, the "Barracks Solution". It sounded ominous. "Actually the Olympic village has been mentioned," he said.

Harriet kept her face utterly still. I had a vision of row upon row of Hon Members squishing themselves into rooms that they would, no doubt, consider fit only for photocopiers. The horror! Not so much Slumdogs as Slumpols. They would hate it.

Sir Christopher, leaning forward, spectacles bookish, voice booming, toyed with Harriet, as a cat does a cornered mouse. What standards of accommodation should MPs expect? For instance, in terms of size? Harriet squeaked that she didn't know. Sir Christopher noted that the Government already had set certain standards on such things in terms of the benefits system and housing allowance. Harriet looked confused. I'm not surprised. MPs would never see their situation as remotely similar.

What about employing relatives, as one third of MPs do? Harriet said that the wives (her word, not mine) worked incredibly hard, 100 per cent, 24/7. "They live the job," said the woman who normally never stops going on about work/life balance.

But was it fair employment practice? Harriet was pale now, her eyes wide. She was asked again. Finally, she allowed that it was a bit like the days when doctors used to employ their wives as receptionists. So? Harriet allowed that it had to stop. I could almost see the words being dragged from her mouth by shire horses as she said: "I think it is almost impossible to convince the public that actually there is fair employment opportunity."

The trawl through the gravy-stain train continued. Was the £7,500 top-up for London MPs a bit high? Why should we pay for family travel costs? Should MPs travel economy on shorter trips? Harriet, meek, mild, had no opinion. Sir Christopher, it seemed, had already wrought a miracle. Harriet had shut up.

18 June

No, really, you were really great ...

This was the last day in the political life of the Speaker, Michael Martin, the man that MPs had insisted must go. But now, of course, they had nothing but praise for him.

Michael Martin ended his speakership as he began it, with a

chip on his shoulder. Over the years, I have watched this calcify and grow until now it is almost the size of Greenland. Thus yesterday, rocky outcrop protruding from robes, the Speaker led the tributes to himself with the gusto of a wronged man.

MPs listened intently, as you must when you are at the leaving do of someone who has been fired but who is in denial. His message was simple: "I was right!" Gordon Brown, the man who had pulled the plug, looked haggard and drawn. He watched warily as Mr Martin upbraided him for not showing more leadership on expenses. Mr Brown will no doubt make amends in the traditional way: the peerage, we must assume, is in the post.

It was, at times, excruciating.

Almost everyone began with a reference to having taken part in whisky tastings for what would become Speaker Martin's Malt, bottles of which are now on sale. It seems an unfitting tribute to a teetotaller but, hey, little falsehoods were the order of the day. MPs then talked about how he was a Roman Catholic, played the bagpipes, loved his wife Mary, grew up in poverty, threw great parties and was kind to everyone, including kittens.

Then they quoted Robert Burns.

Indeed it wasn't so much a Burns night as a Burns smite. Not against Mr Speaker, obviously, but against his foes, the fancy-pants London-based metrosexual lily-livered media.

"We totally deprecate the grotesque anti-Scottish, anti-Glasgow, anti-working class caricature invoked by some London-based newspapers," foamed Angus Robertson, of the SNP, before, yes, quoting Burns (A Man's a Man for A' That).

The theme of a Great Man Wronged was underscored by

Mark Durkan, the SDLP leader. "It happens in life. Sometimes events, perceptions, moods conspire to result in some necessary unfairness or unfair necessity. You find yourself in many ways a victim of that." He added: "In politics irony is just hypocrisy with panache."

Ironically, perhaps, the most panache was shown by the likes of Sir Nicholas Winterton. He and his wife, Ann, are known as Mr and Mrs Expenses. He gushed his gratitude to Mr Speaker for allowing them to use his "wonderful state apartments" to celebrate their 60 years of combined service. "It was a wonderful occasion! You remained to the bitter end to what was a very long party and you were able to do that with humour and commitment without the stimulation of any alcohol whatsoever!" he cried. "I think that indicates the sort of man you are!" Indeed. We then had a bit more Burns (Address to the Unco Guid and a bit more A Man's a Man for A' That.) Throughout the near-two hours of tributes, the tiny figure of John Ber-Cow, Speaker wannabe, had been pogo-ing up and down in a desperate bid for attention. Finally, the Speaker granted his wish.

Mr Ber-Cow enunciated every word and sometimes every syllable. "Almost from Day One you were subjected to a relentless snobbery and disdain from a section of the tabloid press who seemed to think that the election of the son of a merchant seaman represented some sort of constitutional outrage. Sir! That was always far more a reflection on them than it ever was on you!" Pass the sickbag. Mr Speaker, who had been shaking hands Godfather-style throughout, ended by saying that he felt like the man at a farewell dinner who, after the tributes were paid, said: "I didn't realise how much you liked me. I think I'll stay on!" Laugh? They did, so hard they almost cried.

19 June

Town no longer nuts about Hazel

Would little Hazel Blears survive her deselection meeting? Indeed, would we ever even see the woman known as Chirpy Chirpy Cheep Cheep again?

To deepest Salford, then, for the deselection meeting for Hazel Blears. The media vans with their huge satellite dishes started gathering in the afternoon outside Salford Civic Centre, a handsome old brick building surrounded by lawns and begonias.

Out on the corner, I found Steve and Adam from the local radio station ogling the vans. They said that this was the biggest thing to happen in Salford since the Happy Mondays announced that they were re-forming.

A bride, with some really rather impressive tattoos, stood to one side, clutching a bunch of white roses. She was clearly heading for the register office, not the meeting.

Wow, I said to Steve, I haven't seen tattoos like that before on a bride.

They glanced at me. "Get used to it. This is Salford!" So it was. The fabled location of Hazel's grass roots. When she resigned as Communities Secretary wearing her "rocking the boat" brooch on the eve of the elections two weeks ago, she said that she wanted to return to her roots.

The only problem? It turned out that the roots were not so keen on her. Indeed, every voter I talked to yesterday wanted her out. "Disgusting!" said one woman. "So dishonest!" But, I said, she had apologised. No one cared. One Labour Party member had e-mailed a local magazine about the meeting: "I have a broken ankle but I will be there. I want her gone."

Still, everyone seemed to think that she would survive. The meeting was shrouded in mystery. The only thing we knew was that it was set for 7.30 pm and 44 Labour Party members would be there.

By 6 pm a protest of sorts was forming outside the civic centre. Overhead, storm clouds gathered, rain spitting down on the raggle-taggle mix of Unison workers, Socialist Worker types, the odd ordinary person, dog-walkers and passers-by. It was a bit like the human form of an odd-socks drawer.

One Unison worker took a picture of colleagues, huddling together with their home-made signs. "Try to look angry!" he cried to giggles.

When Hazel ran for deputy leader of the Labour Party her slogan was "Nuts About Hazel". Now the placards read "Hazel is Nuts!". Someone from a youth group arrived with manacles, saying that he planned to stage a citizen's arrest under Section 24a of the Police and Criminal Evidence Act for theft by way of deception.

"Hazel, Hazel, Hazel! Go, go, go!" cried the protesters in sporadic bursts. I felt that Iran could teach us a thing or two about protests.

I asked one woman if she had liked Hazel before the expenses scandal. "She was never here," she said. "It was easier to get an appointment with Elvis."

The minutes ticked by. Where was Little Hazie? The protesters and photographers ran around the centre to the various entrances. Surely, I thought, Hazel would want to go in through the main door, head held high (well, as high as possible when you're 4ft 10in). Hazel may be many things but I never took her for a coward.

Rumours swirled. Maybe Hazie was, indeed, in the building.

But how had she got in? "Well, she is rather small," noted one protester. Indeed she was so small that she was invisible all night long. Indeed, as I write at 11 pm, the meeting having ended a half hour ago, I still have not seen one strand of her red hair. The rumour was that she had won by 31 votes to 13. The woman known as Chirpy Chirpy Cheep Cheep was suddenly come over all shy. She is, it seems, no longer rocking the boat.

23 June

A truly irritating victory

MPs can be trusted to make the wrong decision on most things and, for me at least, this proved the case when it came to the Speaker.

In the end, the most irritating man won. Even in victory, John Ber-Cow, as even he calls himself, provoked disharmony.

"Colleagues," he said as if they were all working at Sainsbury's. Labour looked on lovingly, the Tories angrily. "You have just bestowed upon me the greatest honour."

Or, to be more accurate, Labour MPs had. Ber-Cow had been the anti-Tory Tory and, because of that, he was the one that the Labour Party wanted. When the result was announced, on the dot of 8.30 pm, after six hours and three ballots, Labour MPs erupted in a deafening clatter of applause — a rare sound in the chamber — and an instant standing ovation.

Across the way, Tories, the winner in their midst, sat on their hands and bums.

It was embarrassing though Ber-Cow, glowing, probably did not care. Sir George Young, the loser, whose crime had been to go to Eton, was the epitome of good sportsmanship, elegantly flapping his hands together from the start. Few followed.

Finally, David Cameron urged his party to stand up, but not all did.

Ber-Cow was "dragged" to the Chair in a thoroughly unconvincing manner by his "colleagues" Sandra Gidley, a Lib Dem, and the wildly eccentric Tory Charles Walker. As the tiny Ber-Cow stood under the canopy, a Labour MP shouted: "Stand up!" But there was another shout too. "Not in my name!" shouted Nadine Dorries from the Tory benches. Ber-Cow glowed more.

What a day! I don't know why anyone was surprised really. After all, the final choice was clear. Ber-Cow is a bumptious, condescending, patronising man who speaks. very. slowly. so. we. can. all. understand.

Sir George Young is fluent, elegant, experienced. I think we should have known who would win.

But, as one MP said, in despair: "How is it that we are going to end up with an eccentric little troll?" That is the question. Well, no one cannot say it was a decision taken in haste.

It had been a marathon. As the Longest Day in Democracy carried on, MPs began to have a glazed look. If they made a film about this it would be called it "They Shoot MPs, Don't They?" And, of course, these days in Britain, we do.

It had begun giddily, like a school sports day devoted to egg-on-face races. First there were speeches. These were, in general, a lark. Exceptions were too screechy (Ann Widdecombe makes fingernails on blackboards seem soothing) and too narcotic (Madge Beckett). My favourite line was Sir Michael Lord: "Before entering Parliament, I was an arboriculturist. I know the value of tending and nurturing irreplaceable plants."

Indeed. Then the voting began at 3.39 pm. And about 5.30 and 7.10ish. This voting system is called "exhaustive ballot" and we all could see just how knackering it was.

Even by the second vote, most MPs, plotting in groups, made no sense. The losers roamed among them, genuinely distraught. Politics is cruel.

"I think I'll go have another drink — or two," said one MP, face long, body posture screaming "despair", after the first vote, as he pulled out his crib sheet and concluded Ber-Cow would win.

Another MP, slumped against a wall, said: "I'm going to sleep until the next vote."

Sleep. Drink. Gossip. Vote. That was the pattern of democracy at work. In terms of organisation, we were in brewery and p***-up territory. "I remind Members that they should vote only for one candidate," noted Alan Williams, the ancient mariner Father of the House, drily. MPs laughed uproariously.

As I write, the Queen is agreeing to Mr Ber-Cow as Speaker and Tories are already plotting against him.

24 June

New Speaker's trainbearer empty-handed

The new Speaker presided over his first day — in a suit and a simple robe! So where, I wondered, did this leave his trusty trainbearer.

The sing-song cry of "Speeaaaakkkerrr" echoed for seven full seconds at 2.28 pm. In the Central Lobby, several hundred people stood, hushed, waiting for the new Speaker. Like the celebrity he has become, he had banned all photos.

"Hats off strangers!" cried a policeman. John Bercow arrived, walking slowly behind the Serjeant at Arms with her fiery hair and golden mace. He was wearing a suit and — gasp

— a tie of sky blue. I don't even think it was a new tie: I've seen it before. Over the suit he wore a plain black robe. The twiddly bit on the back (this is a technical term) had been excised overnight. He looked a bit as though he was wearing a "Judges' Dressing-Up Kit" for children.

The trainbearer walked behind, looking lost. What's the point of a trainbearer without a train? It struck me that the very first thing the new Mr Speaker must do is give this man something to carry. As this is Britain, why not an umbrella? Or, as Mr Bercow has vowed to clean up Parliament, a pooper-scooper? I suppose, if you were being literal, he could carry a toy train engine.

I ran to the chamber to see the Dawn of a New Era. Indeed, such is the hope invested in Mr Speaker that we may now date all political changes from now as AB (Anno Bercow). He looked rather swamped by the large chair that has fringy bits hanging from its canopy. (If Madge Beckett had won, it would be festooned with all those hanging baskets that we bought her.) It all seemed a bit Mad Hatter's Tea Party. His feet barely touched the floor.

I was on high alert for the Bercow revolution and can report that his first, historic words, were: "Order! The clerk will now proceed to read the title of the private Bill set down for consideration this day." There was a frog in his throat. Labour MPs went to his side to kiss his ring. The Tories eyed this suspiciously.

The revolution began with a question about Men's Health Week. Mr Bercow told everyone to be succinct which, of course, they weren't.

The Labour MP John Robertson praised Mr Bercow and wondered why men don't go to the doctor. Ann Keen, a Health Minister, praised Mr Bercow and agreed that men are notoriously bad at going to doctors. We heard that NHS Choices (what is that?) and the Football Foundation, enlisted for obvious reasons, had highlighted five important male "issues": testicular cancer, skin cancer, mental wellbeing, prostate cancer and sexual dysfunction. Oh dear. The Bercow Revolution was getting off to a ropey start. I had no idea such "issues" would exist in the AB Era.

Now, just to make a queasy situation worse, Andrew Lansley, aged 52 and the Shadow Health Secretary, began to flirt with Mr Speaker, aged 46.

"You know you're getting old when the Speaker looks young," he said, with a flick of his eyes.

Mr Speaker looked coy. He told MPs that he didn't want any more praise. At 4.30 pm he got up and left the chair. I can see why we're paying him £141,866 a year. This revolution business is hard work.

25 June
A three-second wonder

The new Speaker at his first Prime Minister's Questions managed to control the madness for three entire seconds. But, as soon became clear, this day belonged to Dave.

I would love to know what Johnnie Bercow thought of his first PMQs, sitting there in his outsized chair, all proud and puffed up, like a brand-new teacher on his first day.

"I apologise for interrupting the Prime Minister," he chirped at one point, adopting a crouching position that looked as if it owed something to t'ai chi, "but there is simply Far. Too. Much. Noise." That go-slow punctuation is going to drive us all mad.

"The public does not like it and neither do I!" Is that true? I'm not so sure. (I feel for the public, if Johnnie is now their "spokesperson"— or, more accurately, spokes-cow.)

His words stopped the screaming for at least three whole seconds but then, for the first time in ages, David Cameron was on fire and it's quite something to watch.

Dave, too often too clever, kept it simple. He noted that the Prime Minister had said last week that capital expenditure would grow until 2012 but that the figures showed that it wasn't true:"Will you correct what you told the House last week?"

I know, I know. It sounds pretty tame (OK, mind-numbingly dull) but Mr Brown — exhausted, eyebags like shelves — clearly hated it. For our Prime Minister there is no topic as fascinating as "Government Capital Expenditure, 2009 to 2012". It is his special Mastermind subject and, possibly, worth dying for.

He shouted: "Even in real terms a comparison with 9992 (sic) when you were in charge of advising at the Treasury, we are investing 44 billion, you were investing only 16!" That is verbatim. Mr Bercow, legs crossed, test-pattern tie vibrating, watched as Tory backbenchers went wild. It did seem rubbish. For starters, in 9992 (is this the new Gordonean calendar?) Mr Cameron was a junior special adviser, more bag-carrier than guru. To me, though perhaps not you (I will need to check with your spokes-cow), the comparison seemed befuddled.

But then this argument, like so many between other married couples, was not about the subject at hand. It was about Dave humiliating Gordon. "If you believed in transparency and honesty and truth in public life," crowed Dave, "you would get up and say I'm sorry, I've got it wrong! Now do it!" The words "Now do it" stabbed like a red-hot poker. Gordo emitted a cry of pain about Tory cuts. Dave chased after him with the branding fork, his backbenchers screeching their support.

Behind Gordo, the benches were mostly silent. The Cabinet looked grim except for Ed Balls, his mini-me clunking fist, who nodded his head up and down so regularly that it will provoke envy among donkeys. (Between the cows and donkeys, not to mention the sheep, a barnyard theme appeared to be emerging.) The battle raged on. "Find that moral compass!" cried Dave, as Gordo threw down his papers and jabbed his finger (can you have a great clunking digit?). As the noise reached Olympian levels, the new Speaker moved into his new t'ai chi crouch.

Little Johnnie looked at Michael Fabricant, the Tory who, in his summer wig, has hair as yellow as husked sweetcorn. "Mr Fabricant, you must calm yourself. It is not good for your health!" But Mr Fabricant is not the only one who should cool down.

The scores? Gordo minus 2, Little Johnnie 1, Dave 2.

30 June

Gordon's green and pleasant land

This, for our Prime Minister, was a great day for it was the day that he unveiled the document, Building Britain's Future which, he thinks, is his masterpiece.

Oh sunny days! I had forgotten, until yesterday, that we lived in Utopia, a green and pleasant land of milk and honey and skill-based opportunity. But we do. Gordon Brown came to the Commons to unveil his vision and to explain how Britain (soon to be rebranded Gordonia) is getting even better. Forget Britain's Got Talent, Britain has Gordon!

It is, simply, marvellous. Oops, I hope that's not too negative.

The Prime Minister was bubbling with good news, not least that the sun has got its hat on, hip-hip-hip hooray. Yes, that's right, Mr Brown is now making the weather, too. It's a brave thing to do in Britain (sorry, Gordonia) but he is exactly that.

He came before us as a visionary but, sadly, unlike Gandhi, he had no loincloth. Gordon's vision has taken a while but then you can't rush these things. The apple does not just fall from the tree (as Newton knows), you have to see it fall. Still, it has been more than 18 months since Mr Brown said that he wanted a vision, not an election. Since then he has been sitting cross-legged, chanting, with his fellow visionary Peter Mandelson (this is a two-for-one vision deal, like Specsavers).

My only cavil is that the name, Building Britain's Future, is, as visions go, a bit clunky. Surely, Gordon was just being modest (as you may know Mr Brown is an expert on modesty and, as he reminded us yesterday, humility). I understand he thought of Paradise Rebranded (Milton, a sub-visionary, would have understood). Or Gordonia — Leading the World.

But, whatever it's called, it is all marvellous and here is why: Everyone has a job. Yes, everyone. There are no skivers in Gordonia. Every youngster will have a skills base whether they like it or not. It is costing a billion and it is not just a pledge but a "guarantee", just like you get with a fridge.

Green Gordonia. Blake (another lesser visionary) may have dreamt up that line about a green and pleasant land but it has taken Gordo to flesh out the detail. Forget the new Jerusalem, now we know this means four commercial-scale carbon capture and storage demo plants. (NB: these are NOT dark satanic mills).

Everyone has a house. It is like The Three Little Pigs for the masses. Over two years we are tripling our investment to create zillions of homes (all of them green, another bit Blake left out) and then we are going to evict all the migrants. In Gordonia, it is local housing for local people. I'm not sure what that means but the Big Bad Wolf may be busy.

Targets are out, personal entitlement (PE) is in. Several people in the Commons asked what the difference was. Mr Brown — so modest — didn't like to say.

Basically, we may all get PE cards — like Tesco Clubcards — to swipe if we want health checks or personal tutors or to "extend our choices". In Gordonia, everyone's choices are always being extended.

Spend, spend, spend. In G-Utopia, spending plans are tedious irritating things that just remind people of the debt (sorry, did I say debt? What I meant was investment opportunities). Yesterday Mr Brown explained that the decision on this was, really, up to the Chancellor (that modesty again).

So there you have it. Isn't it great? The only tiny cloud on the horizon (I'm sure Gordo can remove it) is that no one knows what's happening with the Royal Mail. Still, visionaries don't need the post, do they?

1 July
Labour's royal couple lord it

When, in the June reshuffle, Caroline Flint decided she didn't want to be Cabinet "window dressing", Gordon gave Glenys a call. This is what happened next.

If there is such a thing as Labour royalty — and why not? — then Neil and Glenys Kinnock are it. In this way, the ceremony that took place in the House of Lords was a mere formality, another curlicue, an acknowledgement of what we already knew to be true. Indeed, in some ways, the House of Lords is almost a step down for these two.

Glenys spent her last moments as a commoner getting "robed" in the almost supernaturally grand Moses Room. Across the lobby, in the chamber, behind the bishops, sat the man who used to be Neil Kinnock, and is now Baron Kinnock, of Bedwellty. (Others call him Lord Windbag but they are just jealous.) He sat, his arms wrapped round himself, beaming. He was still except for his mouth, which was, of course, moving. Up in the gallery, I spotted Sue Nye, the gatekeeper for Gordon Brown, lioness of his inner circle, very much Labour family. A few Labour MPs sat on the throne stairs, as random as scatter cushions, paying homage to the golden couple.

Black Rod entered, stick gleaming, followed by Garter King of Arms, whose extraordinary tabard looked as if it had been nicked off a very expensive sofa. Then came a slight figure, topped with a silver-blonde bob, swamped by ermine. She was accompanied by the fiery-haired Baroness Royall, who is also Labour family, used to work for Neil and is now the Leader of the Lords (the gravy train is impressive sometimes, isn't it?).

"Greeting!" cried a man in a periwig, having unrolled a scroll from the Queen. Neil, mouth now shut, possibly with tape, glowed. The periwig introduced "our right trusty and well-beloved Glenys Elizabeth, the Lady Kinnock, wife of the Right Honourable Neil Gordon, Baron Kinnock". Simple folk. Simple titles.

She will be known as Baroness Kinnock of Holyhead. Now came the goodies. She must sit "among the barons". She must "enjoy and use all the rights, privileges, pre-eminences, immunities and advantages" of being among the barons. What could this mean to a couple who, between them, already have six public sector pensions worth an estimated £185,000 a year?

She gave her oath, accent lilting, reading from what looked

like a giant plastic placemat on the dispatch box. I wondered if Caroline Flint, who refused to be Minister for Europe for she is not just window dressing, was watching.

Lady Kinnock made her way out, so nervous that she failed at first to acknowledge the Lord Speaker. Her fellow peers then turned their attention to a subject of great importance to them: incontinence. As one peer decried "bog-standard" incontinence products, Lord Kinnock slipped out of the chamber.

2 July

The day that Mr Brown bought the train-set

The Prime Minister decided, on the very day he bought a franchise, to tour Britain by train. I rang Downing Street for information on his "meet the people" tour. Hah! What was I thinking?

Shhhh! He's on the train. Yes, I mean Gordon Brown. It's top-secret but it's true. I wish I knew more but if I did I'd have to kill myself. Still I tried. My first call about this was to Downing Street, who told me they could not help in any way. I brushed this off. I am a commuter. I expect a total lack of information about anything to do with trains.

Mussolini made the trains run on time. Stalin ruled Russia from his personal train. And Gordon Brown? Well, on the very morning of his Great Train Journey he requisitioned one. Most people are content to buy a ticket; our Prime Minister had to have an entire franchise. It seemed a little excessive (and much harder for the conductor to punch a hole in).

I call Downing Street again. They refuse to tell me anything about his schedule and say that, anyway, I can't go with him. Still, I am not fazed. I'm a commuter. I'm used to being treated with contempt. I hear he's going north and wonder if, like Harry Potter, he will depart from platform 9¾ at King's Cross.

Actually, having just been to PMQs to see Mr Brown on the very brink of his great journey, this may well be the case. Mr Brown seems well acquainted with fantasy numbers. At one point, as he and David Cameron fought over whether total spending is going up or down, Mr Brown announced: "Total spending will continue to rise and it will be a 0 per cent rise in 2013-14!" The Tories, 100 per cent hysterical, guffawed. Mr Speaker, who is usually 0 per cent effective, cried: "Order! Order! The Prime Minister's answer must be heard."

The Tories screeched louder. "That answer gets 0 per cent!" chortled David Cameron, wag that he is. The percentages started flying like arrows on Valentine's Day. Mr Brown accused Mr Cameron of being Mr 10 Per Cent, a reference to cuts. Mr Cameron said that was rubbish and that, anyway, the Prime Minister was Mr 13½ Per Cent.

It's madness but good preparation for the Great Rail Journey. Train passengers (sorry, customers) are used to figures that mutate, the 20.11 that has a 0 per cent delay but never arrives because it has become, magically, the 20.41. In my experience it is quite normal to catch trains that don't exist. The Prime Minister should feel right at home on the railways.

I ring the Downing Street press office for the fifth time. The phone rings and rings. I'm impressed. Such is their omertà that they no longer even answer the phones. The rumour is that Mr Brown may or may not have headed to Leicester. He's going to meet "the people". So far the main person he's met is Nick Robinson, the political editor of the BBC. Still, it's a start.

Here's a theory: Mr Bean is turning back into Stalin. This week, Mr Brown gave us his National Plan. Now he's ruling from a train. (Soon we'll get those tractor production figures in full with 0 per cent rises all round.) Still, if his train is late, at least the company has a great excuse: the wrong sort of Prime Minister was on the line.

7 July
You've been Quango-ed!

This was the day that Dave decided to tango with Quango Britain. He railed against them but when we asked how many he would axe, he was just a little vague.

David Cameron gave us the Quasimodo take on Quango Britain yesterday. Here was a grotesque landscape, a dystopia full of quasi-organisations that breed without control, their bosses on bloated pay, their costs climbing skyward. Quasi-Quango Britain was frightening but also fascinating, a place of excess that made the drunkards in Hogarth's Gin Lane look controlled.

And that was just the acronyms.

No, really, they are actually truly scary. He gave the example of the Learning and Skills Council which, over time, has given birth to eight baby quangos.

Dave listed them: "The AACS, Jacqa, the NAS, the NES, Ofqual, the QCDA, the YPLA and — I promise I'm not making this up — the last one, the SFA." Dave paused for effect. "I'm told the 'S' does not stand for sweet."

This brought the sweetish sound of laughter.

"What a J-O-K-E," spelled Dave, which brought more laughter. I am thinking that, if this prime minister thing doesn't work out for Dave, then stand-up is the obvious place for him. He has the acting gene, as did Tony Blair, whom I believe he sees as a guru.

It was also very Blair to have gone to Canary Wharf, into the steel and chrome jungle where the grandest quango of all, the FSA (not to be confused with SFA), has its very own tower for its 2,000 staff.

At one point this speech was billed as "The Bonfire of the Quangos" and here Dave was, in the belly of the beast, having a rumble in the jungle, a tango in the quango.

What a pity then that Dave bottled it. Oh, he described the problem brilliantly: 790 quangos eating up £34 billion of our money. There must be reform, he said, "to fix our broken politics". (Is it only me, or is that the most irritating phrase ever?) It was when we came to the solution that things got a bit vague. Dave wants to devise a quango virility test to see if what each does has actual merit. It sounded a good idea but, in reality, I felt that we would need at least one quango to devise and carry out this quasi-quango-quality test.

Plus, Dave wants quango transparency. Dave is so clear on the power of transparency these days that he has taken to carrying around a travel-size Windolene with him. His belief in this is almost religious. "The transparency tool is incredibly powerful," he told us as I tried to imagine a transparency tool — like a hammer but totally see-through, perhaps.

Indeed, it is all too powerful to quantify. Dave did not want to do detail about what all of this would accomplish. For, as he explained, it wasn't helpful to give out any actual numbers.

"On the numbers," he explained, "disappointing as it is for the media, I'm sort of determined not to go down what other politicians have done, the big list, the 10 per cent off or the 20 per cent off approach."

Hmmm. Dave explained that, instead, he is going to do something even more radical. "Much more important is to get the argument right! Once you have got the principles right and you know what you are trying to do, everything else will follow."

Everything else will follow. What did that mean? Dave looked even more pleased and said "very big numbers" would be involved. I'm sure you will agree that that is very impressive, if utterly non-transparent, as in totally opaque, as if we were living in a shoebox. Does this sound like a serious plan or was it, I wondered, a J-O-K-E?

8 July

Metaphor madness as Mandy keeps off the grass

This session with Lord Mandelson began with an indecorous joke and moved on to all things to do with lawns. If I hadn't been there, I wouldn't have believed it happened.

I am sorry to lower the tone, particularly as I am writing about Baron Mandelson of Foy and Hartlepool, but I fear his session with MPs yesterday began with a willy joke.

The subject was that of the Baron's many titles, which are far too many to recount here but include that of First Secretary.

Peter Luff, the rather peppery chairman of the Business Select Committee, noted that Margaret Thatcher had famously remarked that every Prime Minister needed a Willie (as in Whitelaw, her wise adviser). "So are you this Prime Minister's Willie?" demanded Mr Luff.

There was a pause that stretched to the horizon. Lord Mandelson, eyes hooded, face as still as a statue, began to feign a splutter. "I ..." he said, a giggle rippling through the packed room. "Um. I am tempted to extend that metaphor ..." The titters turned to guffaws, "but decorum ..." Decorum? I hardly think that comes into it. The Empire of Mandelsonia, recently expanded to include Outer Space, is a robust place and the good lord, as was obvious yesterday, is totally in control. Indeed, as I watched him twist the committee round his finger, it was hard not to marvel.

Brian Binley, an overexcitable Tory, tried to quiz him on his many roles and whether it was true that, as one newspaper had reported, he'd had a bust-up with Shaun Woodward, the erstwhile Tory who has been advising Gordon Brown on political strategy.

"I don't know quite what you are talking about ..." said Lord Mandelson, affecting an air of mystification. He then told us, for no apparent reason, that he spends 80 per cent of his time running his department and 20 per cent on Cabinet business.

Mr Binley waved the cutting. Was this mere gossip? "It is not only frivolous, it is also trivial and gossip masquerading as journalism. I don't recognise any of these accounts," said Mandy.

I took that to mean it was true.

"Complete fiction!" he fussed. Then I knew it was true.

Mandy spent most of the session speaking in some kind of code involving grass. Yes, that's right, grass. This cropped up (sorry) first when he was asked when he would be able to publish the report into the collapse of Rover, now being examined by the Serious Fraud Office. "There is no question of this report being put in the long grass — it is a pretty closely mown lawn."

I observed the Baron, who is allowing his temples to grey more than usual. Surely his hands, manicured and soft, had never touched a mower.

The discussion turned to Mandy's move partially to privatise the Royal Mail, now stalled until "market conditions" improve.

Lindsay Hoyle, a Labour rebel, wanted to know what was up with the Bill. "Is it in the long grass or is it on the well-manicured bowling green?" Mandy, as silky as his tie, said that it was in neither. Mr Hoyle interrupted: "A bit of rough, is it?" The manicured hands came together. "We are in the hands of the markets here and as markets cheer up ..." Mr Hoyle persisted. "You said you weren't on the bowling green but you weren't in the long grass. So when will you get the mower out and trim the grass?" Get the mower out? This was metaphor madness. Mandy preened: "I hope that you will be able to get out of the rough and towards the velvet lawns of the bowling green as soon as possible."

Everyone giggled. What does it mean? I think that, in Mandelsonia, the grass is always greener — by decree.

9 July

Prudence has given birth to two ghastly children

The Chancellor told us about his new financial system which was, he said proudly, both micro-prudential and macro-prudential. So that's all right then.

I am sure that Alistair Darling read with interest the news that scientists have created synthetic sperm. The Chancellor probably feels as though he has been trying to do something similar in coming up with a new financial system just like our old deeply human system but not, somehow, prone to failure.

Yesterday he came before us to show us his Petri dish. He looked proud, which is to say that his eyebrows wiggled more than usual.

He told us that his plan was bold, counter-cyclical and,

crucially, micro-prudential and macro-prudential.

Can I just warn you that everything now is about macro-prudential? In the good old days (which we now know were very bad), we just had Prudence. But now she has given birth, possibly with the aid of synthetic sperm, to two ghastly children, Micro-Prudential and Macro-Prudential. Surely this is an argument for birth control.

Mr Darling, who with his jet black eyebrows and snow white hair, looks bonkers enough to be a Nutty Professor, at times spoke in total jargon. "The principle of leaning against the cycle is easy to agree," he noted. Oh, I thought, stop showing off in front of Macro-Prudential.

Mr Darling's new synthetic system is quite ingenious. Basically he has taken the old tripartite system (the Treasury, the Bank of England and the FSA) and created a new tripartite system with the exact same trio. But he has given it a new name and is going to give birth to it legally, in Parliament.

I could see George Osborne sneering. If Mr Darling is a drone (and he is), then George Osborne is a sneer.

He condemned Mr Darling's plan. George, who has his own Petri dish, wants a new tripartite in which the Bank, whose governor Merve the Swerve is George the Sneer's new best friend, would be more important and would be given custody of Macro-Prudential (who is, I think we can agree, quite a handful).

Will any of this happen? Only the mad scientists know for sure.

14 July

Cometh the hour, cometh the Jobsworth

The new Defence Secretary was thoroughly unconvincing, not to say uninspiring, when he tried to defend the number of helicopters in Afghanistan.

Bob Ainsworth is one of those people who should never rise above deputy. I am told that people are snobby about him but I am just confused. Every time I see him — and it happened again yesterday — I cannot believe he is the Defence Secretary. How did this man, stodgy as porridge, inspiring as a cabbage, get the top job? It feels wrong, as if he was taking part in a job-swap reality TV programme that has gone horribly wrong.

On a day like yesterday, with Afghanistan the urgent subject, it feels almost unpatriotic to point this out. But there it is. Cometh the hour, cometh the man and in Mr Ainsworth we have a Bob Jobsworth. Apparently he is the first man with a moustache (not sure about the women) in the Cabinet for 40 years. This, I fear, is the most interesting thing about him.

The first question came from a wild-haired Tory, James Brokenshire, who began with a tribute to the fallen. "In those immortal words, for our tomorrows, they gave their todays." Then he looked at Mr Ainsworth: "Why do you think the current helicopter cover is sufficient?" The man masquerading as Defence Secretary said: "We have as we've said repeatedly seen a huge uplift in helicopter frames available to commanders and also helicopter hours. In the past few years, an 84 per cent increase. There will be more. By the end of the year we will have Merlin in theatre and we get the eight Chinook, some of them, out into theatre in 2010."

What does it mean? In reality, on the ground? The date of 2010 echoed in the chamber. Uplift or no, it seemed for ever.

Now came a question from the lugubrious James Arbuthnot, the gloomiest man in Parliament and the Tory head of the Defence Select Committee. "When the Chancellor said the Ministry of Defence would not be short of money, what did he mean?" The moustache bristled. I feared what was coming, for Mr Ainsworth cannot even explain what he thinks, much less someone else. Sure enough, this was his reply, verbatim: "He meant for example that he has lifted the UOR ceiling that was announced in December of 635 million to include another 101 million in order that we get the latest capability into theatre to deal with the UOR process. Everything that we need for this theatre we will present."

Do you feel inspired? Even if you knew that UOR stood for Urgent Operational Requirements, would you? I watched in frustration. It's not that Mr Ainsworth is not box office. It's not that his flat Coventry accent is so banal, so nasal. It's the words that irritate, smothering any meaning in layers of dough.

Liam Fox, who is shadowing his fourth Defence Secretary, looked like he might explode. "When the Government cut the helicopter budget in 2004 by £1.4 billion, was it a mistake?" The Defence Secretary (I was beginning to believe it was him) now became Rambling Bob. "You go back to a decision that was taken some time ago," he noted. "We have made great strides to increase helicopter availability and capability." Mr Fox, steam coming out of ears, snapped: "I'll take that as a yes." He said people understood that in wars there are fatalities but what they didn't understand was why we didn't give our troops the best equipment, including helicopters.

Mr Ainsworth said that Mr Fox was asking for the impossible to be done. But surely, in many ways, that is what Afghanistan is all about. Let's just hope the troops didn't tune in.

16 July

Fiddling while Helmand burns ...

Prime Minister's Questions took place against the backdrop of news reports showing draped coffins from Afghanistan. The political battle was fierce — and fraught with danger for all.

At Prime Minister's Questions, there are lots of fake rows — with much screaming and crashing of crockery — and there are the much rarer real ones. Yesterday David Cameron and Gordon Brown had one of the latter: voices serious, pitch low, content freighted with anger and frustration. The subject was helicopters in Afghanistan and it was dangerous territory for both men.

It's not a new row but, in such a week as this, it felt very raw. The risk for Mr Cameron, in choosing this subject, was that he could look as if he was scoring political points over the draped coffins of our troops. But the risk for Mr Brown was the same, for his clunking-fist style just doesn't suit such vexed matters. It was the last PMQs before the summer break when both men, I suspect, will be reading the military memoir of the moment, The Junior Officers' Reading Club, on Afghanistan.

Mr Cameron began softly softly, saying that it was time to show more visible progress: "We will take people with us for the future if we admit to some of the things we got wrong in the past."

Mr Brown's jaw set. He does not do sorry, as we all know.

Dave dived in: "Isn't the basic problem this: the number of helicopters we have there is simply insufficient?" Was it true that the US Marines, who had the same number of troops, had

100 helicopters while we had fewer than 30? "That is the case, isn't it?" The Prime Minister emitted a torrent of words, none of them answering these questions. He said that the number of helicopters had gone up by 60 per cent in two years. Military men, he noted, say that the deaths were tragic but could not have been prevented by helicopters.

"You talk about a 60 per cent increase," said Mr Cameron, voice steady, "but that is compared with three years ago when we had half as many troops, so there isn't a proportional increase."

The Prime Minister said that, actually, in the past two years troops had gone from 7,000 to 9,000. "The number of helicopters has gone up 60 per cent — now that is a higher percentage rise."

This brought Tory unrest. The PM repeated his numbers to more muttering. How I hated this wrangle, for, to me, it feels like we are fiddling with figures while Helmand burns.

And, on the subject of fiddling, I later found out that both men technically were right about troop numbers (I am told that we had 3,300 troops in 2006, up to 5,500 in 2007, then 8,100 in 2008, and 9,000 now). But, as the MoD won't confirm the number of helicopters, the actual percentages remain unknown.

I am sure that I am not alone in feeling trapped in a spider's web of figures.

Mr Cameron battered on, asking if it was true that since the international helicopter fund was announced 16 months ago, it had not added even one machine. Mr Brown, visibly frustrated, nearly in wounded bear mode, snapped that three helicopters had arrived or were about to arrive from the fund.

"I'm not complacent," said the PM, adding that he believed he was making the "provision necessary" for helicopters.

"Absolutely no answer!" exploded Dave, who had a pop at

the new Defence Secretary, Bob "Jobsworth" Ainsworth, pointing out that in seniority he was ranked 21 out of 23 in the Cabinet (I'm only surprised it's not 23).

The PM snapped back: "I'd hoped this debate could have escaped party politics and partisan points."

This brought outrage, for it was, in itself, a party political point. It really was a most unedifying row. Holiday, anyone?' I am sure I am not alone in feeling trapped in a spider's web of figures'

21 July

You're hired! Baron Sugar takes his seat

Some lords and ladies seemed less than thrilled when Sirallun, the new celebrity enterprise czar, joined them on the red benches.

It was Sirallun's big "you're hired" moment. I can't say the House of Lords as a whole was too thrilled about it. The Tories, in particular, looked rather queasy although, as it was after lunch, some of that could just have been indigestion.

The galleries were mobbed. It is not every day that a celebrity is made a peer; indeed, it may not be any day but this. Sirallun may turn out to be our most famous peer ever. Of course, there are quite a few infamous ones.

Many are outraged about the clash of roles between being the star of The Apprentice and Gordon Brown's "enterprise czar". Sirallun says he's neutral, but others think he's labouring the point.

The chamber looked beautiful. The fairytale throne was gleaming, the candelabras towering, the benches glowing red. I could see that the Tory benches were emptier than usual. On the Labour side, Lord Levy, not seen so often in this place since all that hoo-ha over peerages, was clambering over others in his anxiety to get the best vantage point to see his friend.

A hush fell over the chamber.

First came Black Rod. Then a man known as Garter King of Arms, whose entire upper body is encased in an extraordinary heraldic tabard that made him look like a posh and rather chunky playing card. Then in tripped Sirallun, shorter and slighter than expected, his head sleek (he'd had a haircut) and his stubble so short that it was hardly a five o'clock shadow.

"Greetings!" said a man in a periwig, who began to read out a scroll from the Queen. Sirallun stood next to him, ermine fluffy, robe gently swaying. Directly behind him sat three grim-lipped Tories. As Mr Periwig told us about "our trusty and beloved" Sir Alan Michael Sugar, one Tory slumped forward into what looked like the emergency brace position onboard an aeroplane.

His title was read out: Baron Sugar, of Clapton, in the London Borough of Hackney. The man in the brace position struggled back into an upright posture.

Why Clapton? "I struck my first business deals on the streets of Clapton as a 12-year-old boy by collecting lemonade bottles for the 1p deposits," he explained afterwards, "and sitting on the main road asking for a penny for the guy." It was a rag-to-riches story, and a sentimental choice. Lucky old Clapton!

Lord Sugarpuff, as he will surely become known, was accompanied by two supporters, Lady Vadera and Lord Davies of Abersoch. Both work for Lord Mandelson, the dark über-baron and ruler of all. The fact that both of his "supporters" are on the government payroll is considered suspect. Doesn't he have any other friends who are not being paid to be there? I think we know the answer. I wonder who his "supporters" will be on his updated coat of arms? Apparently, and incredibly, instead of unicorns he could pick Nick and Margaret from The Apprentice.

Now Sirallun — it will take me a while to stop saying that — read out his oath from the plastic placemat on the dispatch box. His eyes flicked up only once towards the Labour benches. The deed had been done!

He bowed his head to the Lord Speaker and processed over to shake her hand. The cheers that followed were distinctly muted and noticeably short. It was more like a momentary bark then anything that could remotely be described as full-bodied. Indeed I didn't see even one Tory mouth open, not even to breathe. The Lords love pomp and circumstance but this, they seemed to feel, was more like pomp and circumspect.

22 July

Life's a swine in Norwich North

The Norwich North by-election was extremely strange: Labour was sick (no, really), the Lib-Dem candidate had a moat and the Tory was too smooth for words.

Just when you thought the Norwich North by-election couldn't get any stranger, it does. Yesterday began with the Labour candidate, Chris Ostrowski, being taken to hospital with suspected swine flu. This left Lord Mandelson (for it is he) at the railway station with no candidate to meet him. Their visit to a Sure Start children's centre, where the teddy bears were all lined up in anticipation, was cancelled at the last moment.

Mandy consoled himself by scuttling over to do a little spinning at the BBC before heading back to London, away from the contagion. As I write, Chris (no one yesterday could pronounce his surname) is at home, in quarantine. The other candidates, who, worryingly, saw him only the night before at a hustings, have sent their best wishes.

It is as if Labour is jinxed here. The by-election was already dominated by a man who wasn't running.

Ian "Gibbo" Gibson, the maverick and beloved local MP, quit in disgust after a party kangaroo court decreed that, because of his expenses, he could not stand for Labour in future. No one has heard from him since, though a shadowy group known as "Friends of Gibbo" claims that he backs Chris Thing.

Who knows? So, yesterday I found myself in Norwich with a Labour void, a Liberal Democrat with the wonderful name of April Pond and the Tory über-smooth wunderkind Chloë Smith.

It is widely assumed that Chloë will win the vote tomorrow, overturning Labour's 5,459 majority. Certainly the Tories have been pouring people in: I even ran into one MP at a service station yesterday on the A11. "Norwichbound!" he trilled at me over the unleaded pump. "We were all told to do four days!"

I was due to see Chloë later but, first, it was off to a printing plant to see the Lib Dem superstar Vince Cable and Ms Pond. Bizarrely, it wasn't even in the constituency. All became clear when I heard April introduce the owner to Vince: "This is my brother, David." It turns out that April has seven brothers and sisters.

She also has a moat. Yes, really. The water theme was hard to escape. It was raining on us as I asked April (surely her middle name should be Showers) Pond about her moat, which I have seen on Google Earth. April, 47, a local businesswoman, points out that hers is a good-luck story. "I was born in a council house and grew up in one with my seven brothers and sisters. I lived part of my life in a caravan in a field." A few moments later she added: "My brother started his life in a drawer in a caravan!" Then it's off to Aquaterra, an oil and gas engineering firm that, as a novelty, was actually in the constituency. Chloë, aged 27, arrives with Ken Clarke, aged 69. They walk around the workshop, minding the generation gap, running out of things to say. Ken looks at a huge round object on the floor. "That looks like a very large screw," he notes sagely.

If Chloë wins, she would be the youngest MP and the only Chloë in the Commons. I find her depressingly machine-like already: smooth, safe, serious. "I am standing as a very clean candidate," she says, looking squeakily so. "I am a fresh face."

Well, up to a point. She is a "business consultant" but, for the past year, she has been working for the Tories in Westminster. "I've never tried to hide that," she says, her voice as smooth as a pebble in a fast-running stream.

23 July
Gordon's holiday horribilis

At the end of his annus horribilis, Gordo tells us all about his plans for a holiday which itself sounded pretty horribilis too.

There were many alarming topics at Gordon Brown's summer press conference — Afghanistan, swine flu, the economy — but by far the most shocking moment came when he told us about his holiday. Would he, like other MPs, be taking off for an 82-day break? "The idea that people are taking 82 days' holiday is wrong," he said sternly, clunking fist crashing down on his lectern as if crushing the life out of summer fun. "I am having a few days' holiday and I am getting on with the job. And other people are having a few days' holiday and also getting on with the job!"

Are they? I don't think so. David Cameron is going to France and Greece. Barack Obama is spending much of August on the island of Martha's Vineyard. Silvio Berlusconi, from what I can figure, is always on holiday.

Still, for Gordon Brown a few days is an improvement on two years ago. Then, as you may remember, he spent only four hours in Dorset (there are rumours that he turned round on the M3) before rushing back to chair a Cobra meeting on foot-and-mouth disease. Last year in Suffolk began badly when he was pictured strolling in his suit but, then, he did seem to relax, building sandcastles with his boys and even taking up Pilates. Plus there was his whirlwind holiday romance with Peter Mandelson (conducted by phone), who was brought back from exile soon after.

But back to this year. What was he going to do? "I am looking forward to a holiday with my children," said Gordo, as formal as a tuxedo, "and it will be in this country."

So a mini-staycation (it is rumoured to be in the Lake District) with the kids but not, it seems, Sarah. I had a vision of Sarah left behind to Twitter to her 440,009-plus followers.

"So any books you want to read?" asked one hack of the PM. My, this was hard work. Still, I leant forward. Mr Brown is a voracious reader, particularly of history. But last week, at the Liaison Committee, when asked about his summer reading, he had announced: "I prefer fiction." I imagined that would be bankbusters, not bonkbusters, but still I wondered what exactly he had in mind.

Now though, he brushed that aside. "As for what I want to

do," he said, "I want to watch a lot of sport."

Watch sport. Fun fun fun, as the Beach Boys would not say. No wonder Sarah's not coming. I had a vision of Gordon and his boys in their cottage in the Lakes. The most beautiful view is on the doorstep but they never see it for they are inside, curtains shut tight, keeping the daylight out, all the better to see the TV.

"This has been a great summer of sport," announced Gordo, "and I have missed too much of it." He'd missed Andy Murray. Then there was the British Lions tour. And the cricket. So a break spent in a darkened room watching sporting repeats on the television. Doesn't it sound ghastly? He may have just lived through a political annus horribilis but this, surely, was a holiday horribilis. Wish you were there? I don't think so.

– ENDS SUMMER –

THE WAKE

The new political year did not so much dawn as crawl on its hands and knees towards what passed for a dawn. Gordon Brown emerged from his "summer holiday" already mired in controversy over his lack of comment on the release the Lockerbie bomber to Libya. Then, Dave stole the agenda, and the battle over whether Gordon could say the "c-word" began. It all felt very much like the beginning of the end, or should that be the end of the end, for Labour.

9 September

Dave's fridge magnet plan

The Conservative leader gathered us together to tell us how he planned to cut the cost of politics and, of course, the shockingly cheap tofu salad at Westminster.

Crisis. Crisis. Crisis. David Cameron began his "I'm back" speech by underlining that we face a grave debt crisis that will only get worse. "The Prime Minister's resolve to do the right thing, to get to grips with public spending, reminds me of one of those fridge magnets — 'The Diet Starts Tomorrow!'"

Dave giggled and the adoring Tory crowd giggled back. I noticed that a midge was buzzing round Dave's head. But, never fear, Dave has a strategy to tackle our alarming fridge magnet slogan crisis. That's why he'd gathered us together at The Imagination Gallery, a fifth-floor glass and steel "space" in Central London that is reached via a metal walkway over an abyss.

The last time I was in this abyss (sorry space) was when Gordon Brown launched his uncontested leadership bid. That turned out nice, as you know. Dave was here to launch his fridge magnet strategy by cracking down on the price of subsidised couscous and chardonnay at Westminster. And that's just for starters (unless, of course, you're on a diet and not having a starter).

Dave is determined to cut the cost of politics. He admitted that public spending on politics amounted to a "pinprick" compared to what is needed, but it's his pinprick. "Those who lead must lead by powerful example," he said as the midge which, surely, is the living epitome of a pinprick, floated ever nearer.

Dave outlined his powerful examples. First he would take a 5 per cent pay cut which, if he were PM, would amount to £6,500. This would obviously be painful for a man worth a reported £30 million.

But, no pain, no gain (as the fridge magnet slogan says) and so Dave is going even farther. "Walk into a bar in Parliament and you can buy a pint of Foster's for just £2.10!" he said. "And in the restaurants you can treat yourself to — I'm not making this next bit up — a lean salad of lemon and lime marinated roasted tofu with baby spinach and rocket, home roasted plum tomatoes and grilled *ficelle crouton* for just £1.70!"

Dave wants that to be more expensive. Actually, I couldn't quite believe he knew what a grilled *ficelle crouton* was. But now he made a face. "I'd pay £1.70 not to have that," he claimed. The Tories giggled. So did Dave whom, if he had regrets so far were tofu to mention now. (Sorry about that.)

"And what about the cars!" he cried. "And I say this as someone who HAS a chauffeur-driven car." He is cutting one third of the cars though not, I noticed, his.

In total, Dave's proposals will save £120 million which, he admitted, when compared to our £175 billion deficit, was "trifling". "This is about more than the money," he announced. "It's about the message." Is it? I thought it was about the money.

Dave suddenly changed tack. "This is £120 million. It's not peanuts!" Well, if it's not peanuts that's because it's marinated roasted tofu.

16 September

The PM has more cuts than Psycho

This speech was billed as the moment when Gordon would say the word "cuts". To date, the only "c-word" we'd heard on Labour lips had been "constraint". But now, in Liverpool before the TUC, Big Gordy was saying the hardest word.

Well, he said it. It wasn't perfect but I was beginning to wonder if he would at all. The build-up was long and arduous. For, like a child who must be bribed before he'll do something loathsome such as eat his peas, Gordon Brown had to have lots of treats first. This involved praising himself with such intensity and at such length that the man behind me fell asleep before we got to the great "cut" moment.

The brothers and sisters of the TUC, who had gathered in Liverpool, were polite as they waited. They had spent a morning debating whether women should wear high heels in the workplace. The Great Stiletto Debate was all about "a woman's right to shoes". Then there was lunch (obviously) followed by Gordon who arrived on stage (wearing flat shoes), kissing everyone like mad, his hair greyer than I remember.

The self-praise began almost immediately, flowing as strongly and surely as the Mersey outside the window. He told us how he'd saved Britain and then the world from a great depression. He listed his achievements including saving 200,000 businesses, enriching 22 million people, saving 500,000 jobs. And, oh yes, something about injecting five trillion dollars into the global economy.

And still we hadn't heard the word. We had five trillion dollars but no tiny little word. Then, as if in a dream, I heard it. "This is not the moment to cut apprenticeships!" he sneered. Oh dear. Right word, wrong context. But it was progress: he was warming up the vocal cords, loosening his inhibitions, getting used to that "kicking cat" sound.

Sadly, he now relapsed, indulging in pages of bragging. Just when I'd given up hope, I heard him say that he would have to "cut" the deficit. Yes, I know, it's not the same thing as saying: "I will make public service cuts", but again it felt like progress.

Now came another mini-relapse (Rome was not cut in a day). "We are doing the right thing," he said, speaking more or less to himself. "As we move into a full recovery we will invest and grow within sustainable public finances — cutting costs where we can." There was that word root again. I felt like shouting: "Go Gordon! You can do it!" He'd been talking for 26 minutes. Eyelids were down all over the room. Then, just one minute later, he exploded. "Labour will cut costs, cut inefficiencies, cut unnecessary programmes and cut lower-priority budgets!" Wow, I thought, feel the quantity. Not one cut but four. Like the proverbial bus, we'd waited for it for ages and now we had more cuts than the Psycho shower scene.

There were no details but then, when such a Herculean effort, you can't expect any. Some people grumped that Gordo hadn't said the word right. It wasn't honest. It wasn't specific. It was just too generic, too vague, too dull.

Duh! And he'd never promised you a rose garden, don't forget, just one word and he'd delivered. More self-praise flowed, then — after 33 minutes, four cuts and about 200 boasts — he stopped.

The brothers and sisters clapped for 45 seconds with a few straggling up to give him a standing ovation which, let's face it, he deserved.

17 September

Liar! Liar! Pants (almost) on fire

Dave stoked the "Tory cuts versus Labour investment" battle with a press conference where he did everything but call Gordon Brown a you know what.

David Cameron began his snap press conference — there really is an election going on, you know — by almost calling Gordon Brown a liar. The word hung in the air, a nearly spoken, lurking presence, the poltergeist in the room. In politics, "liar" is an explosive word. Dave got as far as finding the fuse.

It all began with Dave lecturing us on the New Politics. Basically, as far as I can see, the New Politics are actually just Dave Politics, i.e. the sun is shining, the birds are singing and everything is transparent. "This is about fixing the roof when the sun is shining," he said glibly (I, for one, am completely sick of this phrase, which should be banned).

Dave is excited because there has been a leak at the Treasury (Old Politics equals leaky roofs) and he has got hold of a document that shows that the Government is planning cuts. The Prime Minister has been taunting Dave over his plan to cut, calling him Mr Ten Per Cent. Now Dave is getting his 100 per cent revenge.

"Let me make it clear," said Dave, for in Dave Politics all is clear. "They are not wrong to be planning cuts, but they are wrong to try and cover up their plans for cuts."

Dave fixed us with his big blue eyes. "This is about honesty. It is about trust. This is about not taking people for fools."

Is it? I thought this was about winning an election. Dave has been tantalising us with this line about Gordon and dishonesty for months now. At his June press conference, Dave said: "There is a thread of dishonesty running through his premiership."

Drip. Drip. Drip. And now, of course, a real leak! "So," asked the man from The Sun, "are you calling Gordon Brown a liar?"

Dave, who moments before had told us this was about honesty and not taking people for fools, began to babble.

Gordon had accused Dave of planning 10 per cent cuts but now we all knew that he himself was planning 9.3 per cent cuts (I have to say that Mr 9.3 Per Cent really doesn't have a ring to it).

"It seems as if he was saying one thing in Parliament while his Government was planning to do something different. The words are there. The document is in your hands. He has to explain whether he was being straight or not. That is what he needs to do. I think this is a very important moment. It is a very big issue."

So big, indeed, that Dave was now all shy about it. But, as we left, I swear I could hear the words: Liar! Liar! Pants on fire! Or, as the case may be, pants almost on fire.

21 September

Nick needs to put a socket in it

At the Lib-Dem conference in Bournemouth, Nick Clegg told us that he was electrifying. If only! He seemed totally unplugged to me.

Nick Clegg began his one-man show in Bournemouth by telling us that he was trying to re-create the thrill of his town hall meetings up and down Britain. "It's just been, it's been really, well, in some cases electrifying," he said. The woman next to me, upon hearing the word "electrifying", didn't look up from her Su Doku puzzle. The man next to her kept texting. Across the aisle, I saw a woman's eyes drooping — already!

Electrifying? Is he serious? For Nick Clegg, as he addressed his conference, was not so much live and unplugged, as just unplugged. I'm not sure the national grid could have helped. Or indeed a direct lightning strike. He just doesn't have it in him. What he is good at is being cute (the new hair-cut is a homage to the Tintin quiff). Plus he can do earnest with the best of them. But what he really excels at is rambling. This is a man who can ramble for Britain without even putting on a pair of walking boots.

Take, for example, the subject of tuition fees. When asked whether the Lib Dems would still scrap them, he went on in an answer that felt like an Aboriginal walkabout. Waffle does not even begin to cover it. "We've got to treat people like grown-ups," he insisted, which is political code for I have nothing else to say. "We believe in that policy. I believe in the policy. We want to delivery that policy. But ..." The "but" went on for some time, until a real live Lib Dem who was not doing Su Doku or texting told him that the tuition fees policy was not just about money. Nick called for candour. He didn't have all the answers. Then, as if to prove his case, he said: "Even Vince Cable can't cross all the Ts and dot all the Is." (This seemed odd for there are only two Ts and two Is in "tuition fees").

The world, he noted, had changed. "I accept there is a lot of uncertainty. There is quite a lot of uncertainty around, which we can't do that much about."

At this point the uncertainty included whether this answer would ever end and whether the woman next to me would ever look up from her Su Doku.

Nick told us about his brand-new Fresh Start document. It's all about greener jobs, young people and, he said blithely, as only a Lib Dem could: "The last thing is reinventing politics completely!" But, of course! How easy-peasy that will be. No problem with those Is and Ts. As if on cue he was asked, in this brave new political world, when women would make up 50 per cent of MPs. Mr Clegg agreed the Commons was "very, very kind of male".

Now, suddenly, he changed tack. "We've got some fantastic women in our parliamentary party. Fantastic! Sarah! Lynne! Julie! Jenny! Sandra!" he cried as if hog calling. "We've got lots of other fantastic parliamentarians in both Houses!" He wants more women candidates. "Jo! Jo!" he called. I assumed he was calling out to the young woman MP, Jo Swinson. "Are you here, Jo?" Silence. Jo wasn't here. Or possibly she was and had been electrified. Who knows? Nick babbled on. "Jo tells me one of the biggest barriers [to women running for office] is actually psychological barriers, a lack of self-confidence! We need to be reaching out and saying: You bet you can do it!" Yes, but can he do it? I'm not sure but, when it comes to electricity, Mr Clegg needs to put a socket in it.

2 October
The Wake

The entire Labour conference in Brighton had a fin de siecle feel to it. No matter what Gordon (or Mandy, or Harriet) did, everything just kept going wrong. The last day was positively surreal.

The hauntingly beautiful quaver of the violin wafted over the comrades yesterday as they made ready to leave Brighton. The thread of sound, played by a Labour Party member introduced only as Helen, accompanied the comrades as they sang the Red Flag and then Jerusalem. It was, undeniably, the sound of sadness.

"We'll keep the Red Flag flying here," sang the PM, face wooden, upper lip stiff, standing tall, as if he was in church. He looked out over a hall in which every effort had been made to make it seem fuller. Black curtains had been drawn, blocking out the empty upper tier at the back and sides. On the floor, the empty seats made it look like a colander but the stage was crowded, populated by a strange group of people who included men in hardhats. I'm sure it was done to show diversity but it looked like an invastion of the Village People.

Still, they kept their little red flags flying high here — at least for the day. It felt more like a wake than a rally and I mean that in a good way. Everyone spoke well of the dead. We saw a film about the Labour party — about Jarrow, the NHS, the suffragettes — that had the sentimental sepia feel of a Hovis advert. They watched, eyes smarting.

The comrades can't believe it's over, that it's ended like this. They hate the media. The week had begun with the PM being asked if he took happy pills and had ended with the *Sun* newspaper backing the Tories. The paper is their new villain and, yesterday, a few comrades on the floor took joy in ripping it in up to cheers.

What has struck me throughout the week was how, in general, everyone has improved from a year ago. Gordon's more human, Harriet is funnier, Mandy a force for unity. And yesterday David Miliband was miles better than last year when he seemed to be impersonating a bendy doll, all spaghetti arms and goofiness. This time it was a serious and solid speech though, at times, he appeared to be channelling his inner Churchill.

It was left to Harriet to raise the dead in the traditional end of conference rallying cry. She is more cheerleader than warrior but she did her best, apple cheeks glowing. We've made progress on equality," she said, "even in the *Sun*!"

I saw people flinch at the name. "On page three today there's a young woman who's really concerned about jobs for women as well as men. And what a coincidence — she's called Harriet, aged 20, from Peckham!" This brought more cheers and jeers. "The only problem," said Harriet, aged 59, from Peckham, "is that Harriet is so concerned about jobs that she's forgotten to put her clothes on!"

The laughter was genuine. Harriet now poured praise on Gordon Brown, ladling it on with the zeal of a over-generous hostess. Behind her, Mr Brown, hair neat for the occasion, was impassive as he looked out on the end of an era.

— CURTAINS —

ACKNOWLEDGEMENTS

People always want to know what the collective noun for sketchwriters is and we always say it is a "sneer" though, actually, we call it "the guild". I am grateful to my fellow sketchers: Simon "The Agent" Carr, Andrew Gimson, Simon Hoggart and Quentin Letts. I also must mention the late Frank Johnson. My thanks to all at *The Times* who have helped make this book happen. All the sketches that I have chosen for this book appeared in their original form (almost all have been edited for this book) in *The Times* on the date noted. In particular, I have benefitted greatly from the help of those who work with me in "The Room" at Westminster: Peter Riddell, Philip Webster, Francis Elliott, Sam Coates and Suzy Jagger. I am in debt, also, to the news desk and the sub-editors, Matt Lyons in particular, who save me from myself on a regular basis. Others to whom I am grateful include Ian Berkoff, Paul Dunn, Sandra Parsons and Martin Rynja of Gibson Square Books, whose idea it was.

INDEX

There are four people who you will not find in the index because they appear on so many pages that the whole listing would be like a bar code gone berserk. They are Gordon Brown, David Cameron, Alistair Darling and George Osborne.

"And we are on TV!", 184
"Clearly time for me to move on", 167
"Companies should have a soul", 124
"Fabulous, absolutely", 163
"Hats off, Strangers!", 177
"I'd love to know what she's done with it", 183
"Money to flow to YOU", 114
"Pooled spray", 141
"Quite so", 194
"Real help", 84
"Smell the coffee", 100
"Soak the Rich", 155
"The best time for now is now", 154
"Themba", 140
"Um" Pesto, 99
"Unredacted receipts", 90-91
"We"re doing the right thing", 245
"What a Feminist Looks Like", 122
"Youth champions", 79

Absolutely Ludicrous, 165
Action Man, 168
Afghanistan, 14, 70, 110, 231-33
After-dinner speeches, 119
Ahmadinejad, Mahmoud, 187
Ainger, Nick, 129
Ainsworth, Bob, 195, 229-30, 233
Alfie, 154-56
Annus Horribilis, 8-15
Anram, Michael, 169
Aphalara itadori, 54
Arbus, Diane, 13
Arbuthnot, James, 71
Austin, Ian, 158
Away Day Cabinet, 78

Bacon, Richard, 175
Baker, Norman, 167
Baldry, Tony, 44
Balls, Ed, 173, 217
Bank of Scotland, 40
Barber, Lionel, 98
Beast of Bolsover, The 113
Beatles, 84, 86
Beckett, Margaret, 173, 203, 212, 214
Beckham, David, 66
Being right all the time, 11
Beith, Sir Alan, 203
Bell, Sir Stuart, 44, 56, 176
Benn, Hilary, 22
Bercow, John, 202, 204, 208, 211, 213-15, 215-17
Binley, Brian, 226
Blair, Cherie, 198
Blair, Tony, 9, 41-42, 68, 150, 183, 186-88
Blears, Hazel "Flipper", 7, 12, 19, 170, 172-73, 178, 185, 190, 197, 209, 210-11
Boland, Dave, 26
Bono, 23
Booth, Lauren, 198
Bradford & Bingley, 34, 138
Brent, David, 160

INDEX

Bribery 101, 157
Brown, Nick, 68, 118
Brown, Sarah, 9, 29-31, 48-49, 238
Burnham, Andy, 78
Burns, Robert, 207
Buzz Lightyear, 202
Byers, Stephen, 156

Cable, Vince, 23-5, 40, 111, 113, 236, 248
Caine, Sir Michael, 155
Cameron, Ivan, 110
Camp, 8, 118, 127
Campbell-Bannerman, Sir Henry, 198
Captain Gordon, 86-7
Car crash, 161
Cartland, Barbara, 30, 198
Cash, Bill, 121
Cassio, 179-80
Catatonics Anonymous, 118
Chamberlain, Neville, 118
Churchill, Randolph, 45
Churchill, Winston, 118
Clappison, James, 120
Clark, Greg, 152, 193
Clarke, Ken, 84, 85, 237
Clegg, Nick, 25-7, 111, 157, 170, 171, 247-49
Climate change, 151-2
Clinton, Bill, 140
Clinton, Hilary, 141
Constable, John, 76
Cormack, Sir Patrick, 45, 161, 176, 203
Counter-quoting, 127
Cousins, Jim, 128
Cranmere, Thomas, 44
Crash Gordon, 106
Cromwell, 180
Crosby, Sir James, 104

Daily Telegraph, 14, 165
Dartmouth, Lord, 198
Dave Confidential, 183
Dave Politics, 246
Dave Way, the, 67
Dave's baby, 80-1
Dave's fridge magnet strategy, 242-43
Davies, Lord, 234
Dhandy, Parmjit, 203
Digby-ing, 109
Duncan Smith, Iain, 182
Duncan, Alan "Hunky Dunky", 44, 91, 121-23, 160-61, 169
Durkan, Mark, 208
Dylan, Bob, 93

Eden, Anthony, 118
Edinburgh Jones, 128
Eliot, T.S., 199
Ethical capitalism, 77
Eton, 42
Euro-ranto, 121
Euro-topia, 121

Fabricant, Michael, 217
Fallon, Michael, 52-53, 137
Farage, Nigel, 197
Fauntleroy, Little Lord, 58
Featherstone, Lynne, 24
Ferry, Bryan, 39
Flint, Caroline, 192, 219
Follett, Barbara, 166
Fox, Liam, 230
Fred the Shred, *see Goodwin, Sir Fred*
Frown Launch, 67

G(ordon)20, 59
Galápagos turtles, 90
Gardner, Baroness, 54
Garland, Judy, 37
Gibson, Ian, 236
Gidley, Sandra, 212
Global economy, 12, 14
GMTV, 45
Goodwin, Sir Fred "the Shred", 101-3, 111-13, 119, 123-25, 127
Gordonia, 218-9
Gove, Michael, 169
Grayling, Chris, 145, 169, 189
Great Man Wronged, 207
Great Stiletto Debate, 244
Great Substantive Motion Question, 175
Greaves, Lord, 55
Green custard, 119-21
Greenspan, Alan, 132
Gummer, John, 151
Gurkhas, the 7, 14, 47, 157-59, 161-65, 180-82
Gustav, Hurricane, 18

Hague, William, 111, 117-9, 153
Hain, Peter, 196
Hairshirts, 170-71
Hamlet, 66
Hammond, Philip, 156
Hands, Greg, 194
Harman, Harriet, 90-1, 117, 121-23, 148, 160-61, 178, 193, 203-5, 249-51
Harvey, Nick, 91
Haselhurst, Sir Alan, 203
HBOS, 36, 102, 103, 138
Heath, David, 159
Heathcoat-Amory, David, 186
Hepburn, Stephen, 155
Hewitt, Patricia, 167
Hoey, Kate, 166
Hogg, David, 169
Hohn, Chris, 94
Holiday horribilis, 237-39
Hoon, Geoff, 196, 199
Howarth, George, 158
Hoyle, Lindsay, 227
HSBC, 108
Hughes, Beverley, 78
Hunt, Lord, 54-55, 201
Hunter, Anji, 46
Hutton, John, 22, 196

Iraq, 71

INDEX

ITN, 79

James Lyons, 8
Jenkin, Bernard, 138
Johnson, Boris, 34-35
Jones, Lord, 107-8
Jowell, Tessa, 46, 178

Kaufman, "Dame" Gerald, 178
Keen, Ann, 214
Kelly, Ruth, 32-4
Kelly, Sir Christopher, 160, 204-6
Keynes, John Maynard, 50-1
Kilfoyle, Peter, 156
Kilroy-Silk, Robert, 197
King James Bible, 44
King, Martin Luther, 56
King, Mervyn, 52-3, 132-33, 134-35, 228
Kingman, John, 116
Kinnock, Glenys, 219-21
Kinnock, Neil, 219-21

Landale, James, 164
Lansley, Andrew, 169, 215
Lehman Brothers, 24
Letwin, Oliver, 169
Levy, Lord, 234
Libya, 14, 241
Little Miss Plod, 118
Livingstone, Ken, 35
Lloyds, 36
Lockerbie, 241
Lord, Sir Michael, 203, 212
Love-bombing, 191
Luff, Peter, 106, 225
Lumley, Joanna, 13, 45, 47, 157, 161-65, 180-82

Mackay, Lord, 180
Mactaggart, Fiona, 122
Mahmood, Khalid, 104
Male "issues", 215
Man Who Saved the World, 69, 79, 126, 147
Mandelson, Peter, 7, 43-47, 72, 84, 119-21, 134, 196, 200-2, 218, 225-27, 234, 235, 249-51
Mandy magic, 120
Marr, Andrew, 42
Marshall, Paul, 94
Martin, Michael, 165-7, 174-78, 206-8
Marx Brothers, 163
Masters of the Universe, 102
Maude, Francis, 169
McBride, Damian, 32
McDonagh, Siobhain, 196
McFadden, Pat, 40
McFall, John, 52, 94, 116
McIntosh, Lord, 83
McKillop, Sir Tom, 103
McNulty, Catherine, 49
Mercer, Patrick, 162
Merkel, Angela, 142
Merve the Swerve, *see Mervyn King*
Metrosexual, 42, 207
Miliband, David, 27-9, 118, 141, 150, 172, 250
Miliband, Ed, 150-52, 192
Miners in the government, 127
Minnie Mouse, 184
Mirror, 8, 122
Moat envy, 169
Mole of the Universe, 94
Moral Maze Moses, 139
Moreno, Glen, 115
Morley, Elliot, 174
Moses, 45, 83
Mr Ten Per Cent, 246
Mudie, George, 124-25
Myners, Lord, 82, 117, 123-25, 127, 138

New Dave, 169
New Labour, death of, 149
New Politics, 246-47
Newby, Lord, 83
Newmark, Brooks, 63
Northern Rock, 24, 99
Now For Change, 77
Nye, Sue, 220

Obama, Barack, 56-7, 88-89, 113-15, 129, 140-42, 187, 205
Opik, Lembit, 26, 182
Opus Dei, 33

Paisley, The Rev Ian, 41
Parnell, James, 185
Pearson, Ian, 194
Pearson, Lord, 198
Peston, Robert, 97-99, 108
Peston-itis, 108
Phoney Phil, 164
Pickles, Eric, 153
Pilates, 22, 23, 238
Pitman, Sir Briain, 100
Pond, April, 236
Porn, 13, 137, 144, 146, 191
Potter, Harry, 31
Prentice, Gordon, 175
Prime Minister's Questions (PMQs), 42, 50, 68-69, 84, 95, 104, 110, 117, 126, 215, 222, 231
Prince of Darkness, the, 200-202
Prudential, micro- and macro-, 227-28
Punch and Judy, 51, 85, 105, 126
Purchase, Ken, 161
Purnell, James, 194-95

Quango-transparency, 224
Queasing, 132
Qaeda-al, 70
Queen, The, 46, 141, 163, 195, 213

Randall, Jeff, 99
RBS, 40, 87, 94, 103, 112, 116, 119, 124, 129, 136, 138

INDEX

Redmond, Phil, 78
Rice-Davies, Mandy, 125
Rigby, Eleanor, 194
Robertson, Angus, 207
Robertson, John, 214
Roy, Lindsay, 49
Royall, Baroness, 92, 179, 220
Ruddock, Joan, 192
Rumsfeld, Donald, 133

Saddam Hussein, 10
Sage of Threadneedle, 133
Sarko, 142
Schwarzenegger, Arnold, 35
Scotland, Baroness, 179
Scrooge, 63
Sentamu, Dr John, *see York, Archbishop of*
Seventeen millionaires, 156
Shakespeare, 179
Sharples, Baroness, 54
Shaw, Douglas, 94
Sheerman, Barry, 159
Shepherd, Richard, 204
Sinclaire, Nikki, 197
Sirallun, *see Sugar, Alan*
Skinner, Dennis, 89, 113, 127
Sky TV, 99, 166
Slumpols, 205
Smith, Adam, 139
Smith, Chloë, 236-37
Smith, Jacqui "Bathplug", 7, 12, 68, 144-6, 166, 181, 188-91
Snape, Lord, 92
Soames, Sir Nicholas, 178
Soulsby, Sir Peter, 194
Spelman, Caroline, 153
Spielberg, Steven, 123
Stalin, Josef, 9, 221
Star Trek Green Enterprises, 151-2
Strathclyde, Lord, 92
Stravonia de Montagnac, Nadine, 64-65
Strictly Come Dancing, 23
Stringfellow, Peter, 64-5
Student politics, 96
Sugar, Alan, 13, 185, 196, 201, 233-35
Sugarpuff, Lord, *see Sugar, Alan*
Sun, 250
Sunday Times, 91-2
Swayne, Desmond, 188-9
Swinson, Jo, 249

talkGORDON, 114-15
Taylor, Baron, 92, 179
Taylor, David, 44
Temple of Foam, 128-29
The Manure Parliament, 171
The Scream, 149
The Smile, 150
Times, The, 60, 61
Timms, Stephen, 155
Tintin quiff, 248
Tory scorpion, the, 135-36
Tory Squirocracy, 167
Touch My Bum, 26
Toxic debt, 113
Trains, 222
Truscott, Lord, 179
TUC, 19-20, 244
Turner, Lord, 53
Twitter, 9, 238
Tyndale, William, 44

Uckfee, 116
UKIP, 197-8

Vadera, Baroness, 234
Vanity, 159-160
Vaz, Keith, 60, 158, 161
Video games, cheerful, 115
Viggers, Sir Peter, 132
Village People, 240
Volupts, the, 4, 192

Walker. Charles, 212
Widdecombe, Ann, 170, 204, 212
Willetts, David, 169
Willy joke, 225
Windbag, Lord, *see Kinnock, Neil*
Winslet, Kate, 153
Winterton, Sir Nicholas, 208
Women in politics, 153, 161-65, 189-90, 192-94, 206, 248-49
Woodward, Shaun, 226
Woolas, Phil, 59-61, 157, 162, 164
Wright, Tony, 107, 160, 170

York, Archbishop of, 82
Young, Sir George, 107, 160, 203, 211-13
YouTube, 147-9, 159
YoYo Brown, 186

Zimmerman, Stephen, 94